Start Your Own

NET SERVICES BUSINESS

Additional titles in *Entrepreneur's* **Startup Series**

Start Your Own

Entrepreneur

MAGAZINE'S

startup

2ND EDITION

Start Your Own

NET SERVICES
BUSINESS

Your Step-by-Step
Guide to Success

Entrepreneur Press and Liane Casavoy

EP
Entrepreneur.
Press

Publisher: Jere L. Calmes
Cover Design: Beth Hansen-Winter
Production and Composition: CWL Publishing Enterprises, Inc., Madison, WI

This publication is designed to provide accurate and authoritative information in regard to the subject matter covered. It is sold with the understanding that the publisher is not engaged in rendering legal, accounting or other professional services. If legal advice or other expert assistance is required, the services of a competent professional person should be sought.

ISBN 13: 978-1-59918-260-5
       10: 1-59918-260-2

Library of Congress Cataloging-in-Publication available.

Printed in Canada
13 12 11 10 09   10 9 8 7 6 5 4 3 2 1

Contents

▲

▲

Chapter 6

Make a Plan. **73**

Chapter 7

Making It Official **89**

Chapter 8

Getting Financing **101**

Preface

Internet startups get a bad rap. After all, everyone remembers what happened in the late 1990s, when companies launched in droves, only to burn out quickly—while also burning through millions of dollars. Some of the greatest success stories became cautionary tales, used to warn entrepreneurs what not to do when starting a company.

Who'd want to get involved in that? You—if you're smart. That is, after all, why you're reading this book.

Sure, starting an internet company can be a risky proposition. But it can also be one of the most rewarding—financially, professionally and personally—ventures you'll ever take on. The

▲

stakes are high, but the profits can be even higher—if you go about it the right way.

The dotcom heyday of the late 1990s saw companies launched without business plans—without any plans, really. The only plan they had was to grow as big as they could, as quickly as possible. Profits were an afterthought. Today, we've learned from those mistakes. We know that you need to make money to run your business, and you need a firm plan in place before you get started.

The internet has grown up since the end of the last century. It's a more mature business environment, and there are a host of new technologies available to web surfers and entrepreneurs alike. These technologies—Ajax, RSS feeds, wikis, podcasts and more—have changed the way we use the web. Web surfers aren't simply passive observers; they're now active participants in the sites and services they use. This is the Web 2.0 world.

There are plenty of business opportunities available in this world, and this book will focus on a few of them. Specifically, we're looking at four internet-based services you can start: a web design firm, a search engine marketing firm, a new media company, and a blogging business. These are four very different businesses, but they also have one big thing in common: They have a huge potential for growth.

In the past, many internet companies focused on providing goods, not services. But services are considered by many to be the wave of the future. Consider this excerpt from Tomorrow's Jobs, a report by the U.S. Bureau of Labor Statistics.

"The long-term shift from goods-producing to service-providing employment is expected to continue. Service-providing industries are expected to account for approximately 15.7 million new wage and salary jobs generated over the 2006-2016 period, while goods-producing industries will see overall job loss."

Still not convinced that a net service is the way to go? Consider this excerpt, from the same report:

"Employment in the information supersector is expected to increase by 6.9 percent, adding 212,000 jobs by 2016. Information contains some of the fastest-growing computer-related industries such as software publishing, internet publishing and broadcasting, and wireless telecommunication carriers. Employment in these industries is expected to grow by 32 percent, 44.1 percent and 40.9 percent, respectively."

The numbers are compelling, to be sure. You still may be wary of starting an online business, and that's understandable. After all, you lived through the late 1990s. You saw what happened to all those dotcom startups. Perhaps you even experienced it for yourself. (I know I did. I was hired by a company looking to expand its presence on the World Wide Web in 1998. I—like many of the people who were hired along with me—found my position eliminated about a year later, when the business environment started to get rocky.)

But if you think that all dotcoms eventually went south, think again. Yahoo! and eBay weren't the only survivors of the internet bubble. "Was There Too Little Entry During the Dotcom Era?," a recent report published by the University of Maryland's

Robert H. Smith School of Business, suggests that, actually, a good deal of companies survived. The report contends: "The survival rate of dotcom firms is on par or higher than other emerging industries."

The report states that "Exit rates of dotcom firms are comparable with or perhaps lower than exit rates of entrants in other industries in their formative years. Five-year survival rates of dotcom firms approach 50 percent."

Fifty percent. That's right—almost half the dotcom companies founded during the boom days lived to tell about it. And they did so without the advantages you have now: the perspective that the past decade has given you, a potential customer base that has grown and matured along with the internet, and new technologies that make it easier—and cheaper—to reach that audience. Imagine the possibilities.

—Liane Cassavoy

1

Join the New
Net Revolution

Just a few short years ago, anyone with a sliver of an idea and a domain name could make money on the internet—or so it seemed. The late 1990s saw the arrival of the first internet boom, when dotcom startups popped up like weeds, money flowed freely, lifestyles were lavish and everything was good.

Business plans were optional, as was profitability. Venture capital funds poured in—and often right back out. Many of these dotcom companies didn't actually have a plan to make money; they simply wanted to grow as large as they could, as quickly as they could. The only plan was to gain users on the now widely available World Wide Web, and worry about making money later. After all, if your company was big enough, it would eventually make money somehow—right?

Web-related companies went public in droves, raising incredible amounts of cash. Internet millionaires were made, on paper at least. Entrepreneurs and investors believed this was the start of a new economy—an internet economy—that would last forever.

But nothing lasts forever. In March 2000, the NASDAQ index reached its peak value of 5048, and began its steep downward decline. Internet companies began reporting substantial losses, and many started to close up shop. Investors, entrepreneurs and much of the general public began to realize there were fundamental flaws in this new internet economy. First and foremost, they realized, companies—even dotcom ones—must make money to survive.

Current State of Affairs

Still, many internet companies were able to survive the bursting of the bubble—eBay and Yahoo!, to name two. But for every Yahoo!, there was a Pets.com. The online pet store launched in 1998 and earned its first round of venture capital funding in 1999. So much money came in that the company was able to pay $1.2 million for an attention-grabbing ad (featuring its sock puppet mascot) that ran during the 2000 Super Bowl. But Pets.com didn't last to see the next Super Bowl: After going public in February 2000, the company quickly lost value and closed its doors that November.

Pets.com is an extreme example, but it's one of the many cautionary tales that can scare both entrepreneurs and investors away from the web. Following the dotcom crash, many companies tried to distance themselves from the internet, going so far as to drop the phrase "dotcom" from their names. But today, the internet is essential to all businesses and is accessed in more homes than ever before.

What's Coming Next?

With such a large and varied internet audience, there's still plenty of room for new internet businesses. The widespread adoption of high-speed internet access is especially important to note: The use of

Stat Fact
More than 50 percent of U.S. households with internet access now have broadband service, according to a recent report by the Pew Internet & American Life Project.

> **Fun Fact**
>
> Pets.com may have closed up shop, but the company's popular sock puppet mascot wasn't unemployed for long. An automobile loan provider purchased the rights to the mascot and used it in ads for its service, with the slogan "Everybody deserves a second chance.

broadband is one of the driving factors behind a new wave of internet technologies—and companies that take advantage of those technologies. Often referred to as Web 2.0, this new era of internet innovation is driven by user-generated content. The web is no longer on a par with newspapers or TV; it's not a collection of static pages that users read or shows that they watch. In today's 2.0 world, the web is interactive. Users generate content and share it with others. Users take content from one site and mix it with content from another site, only to post the result on a third site.

Consider the site many consider to be the epitome of success in the Web 2.0 world: YouTube, which allows almost anyone to upload a video and share it with the world. Viewers can then interact with the video by adding their comments or posting it on their own blog, social networking page or personal website. Created in early 2005, YouTube was acquired in late 2006 by Google. The price? $1.65 billion. Yes, that's billion, as in one thousand million dollars.

Your company may not make billions of dollars, but—clearly—there's money to be made on the internet.

Four Internet Services You Can Start

The internet is a vast place; they don't call it the World Wide Web for nothing. There's really no limit to the types of businesses you can start online. This book will look at four types of internet services you can start, often at home, and, in some cases, in your free time. The services we'll discuss are a web design business, a search engine marketing business, a new media service and a blogging business.

Web Design Business

When access to the World Wide Web hit a critical mass in the 1990s, much of the general public got their first look at a web page. And with that, a new industry was born: web design. These days, every business needs—and many individuals or families want—a web page, but they don't know how to create one. They don't know HTML from XML, or JavaScript from AJAX. So they need help.

That's where you come in. You may be an artist who learned how to translate your

Defining Moment

The phrase "Web 2.0" is tossed around so often that it's easy to forget its actual meaning. In fact, some of its critics claim it doesn't really have a meaning at all. To find out exactly what it does mean, we did a little digging.

The phrase was coined by Tim O'Reilly, the man behind O'Reilly Media, a company that publishes user-friendly computer books and hosts technology conferences. Over the years, O'Reilly has become well-known as an expert on all things internet-related. According to a 2005 article by O'Reilly, the term was born during a brainstorming session in 2004. Despite the "2.0" label, the phrase doesn't refer to a new technical version of the web; rather, it denotes a turning point in its history. The turning point, O'Reilly and his colleagues noted, was after the dotcom crash. The crash hadn't stifled internet innovation; instead, it seemed to pave the way for even more of it. In a Web 2.0 world, services are preferred over packaged software, users shape and generate the content they view online, and that content is available across different platforms and devices.

O'Reilly uses examples in his article that help explain the difference between a Web 1.0 site and a Web 2.0 service. For instance, Britannica Online is a Web 1.0 site, while Wikipedia is its Web 2.0 equivalent. In a Web 1.0 world, people had personal websites. In a Web 2.0 world, they have blogs.

Still not sure what it means? The phrase is hard to define, in large part because its meaning is constantly evolving. Something that may be a hallmark of a Web 2.0 company by the time you read this book may not have existed when this book was written. That's just how fast things change in a Web 2.0 world.

sense of style to the web. You may be a computer programmer who knows what looks good and works well online. And you're not alone: Type "web design firm" into Google, and you'll get more than 43 million results. It's difficult—if not impossible—to estimate the actual number of web design companies out there, as the U.S. Bureau of Labor Statistics (BLS) doesn't differentiate web designers from graphic designers in their statistics it collects. Also, most of the directories that list web design firms only put those that sub-

Bright Idea

Is a client looking for a service you don't offer? Don't turn down their business: Hire a contractor. Say you get a request to build a shopping cart, but you don't handle e-commerce services. Find someone who does. You'll want to vet your contractors thoroughly, but setting up this type of arrangement can result in reciprocal business for you.

> **⚠ Beware!**
> Watch out for services that claim to boost your business by listing your company information in their directory for a fee. Sometimes it can pay to become a member of an industry association, but do your homework before forking over the cash. Before you pay up, get recommendations from people you know and trust in your industry.

mit their company info and/or pay for inclusion in the directories.

Suffice it to say, though, there's plenty of competition out there. That doesn't mean you shouldn't consider this a business possibility. In its "Job Outlook" for graphic designers, the BLS predicts that from 2006 to 2016, "graphic designers with website design and animation experience will especially be needed as demand increases for design projects for interactive media—websites, video games, cell phones, PDAs and other technology. Demand for graphic designers also will increase as advertising firms create print and web marketing and promotional materials for a growing number of products and services."

Web design firms vary greatly in size. Some are single-person operations; others are large companies. You can run a web design company by yourself as a part-time gig, while still maintaining a full-time job elsewhere. This allows you to pick and choose only the projects you have the time and the desire to complete. You could also take the plunge and start your business full time, focusing on growing it into a bigger company. We'll discuss all these options in more detail in Chapter 2, which focuses on web design companies.

Web design firms also vary greatly in scope. They may design anything from basic HTML-based web pages for sites with simple navigation schemes to more complex Flash- or AJAX-based sites. Some firms offer services that go beyond simple site design: domain name registration, website hosting, shopping cart implementation, e-commerce functionality and search engine optimization. Other firms focus more on the design aspect and will design not only web pages but also company logos and print marketing materials, like brochures and company letterhead.

The focus of your web design business will likely depend on your background and skill set as well as that of any partners you may bring on board. And that's the way it should be: With so much competition out there, you need to leverage your expertise to set your company apart.

Search Engine Marketing Service

Search engine marketing, or SEM, is one of the most buzzed-about terms on the internet. And for good reason: It's a rapidly growing industry. According to MarketingSherpa's Search Marketing Benchmark Guide, the search marketing industry grew by more than 31 percent in the United States in 2007. Globally, growth was at 39 percent. The guide notes that "search budgets are increasing by double-digit percentages." Clearly, companies are willing to spend money on SEM, and there's money to be made in this field.

But what exactly is SEM? The term is often used together with the term "search engine optimization" or "SEO." Some people use the words interchangeably, but they're not synonymous.

To understand the differences, it's

Stat Fact

Just how dominant is Google? It's used for nearly 60 percent of all web searches, according to a recent survey by comScore Video Metrix, a digital researcher. That's nearly three times as many as its nearest competitor, Yahoo!, which handles almost 23 percent of web searches.

helpful to understand how search engines work. And because it's by far the most popular search engine out there, we'll focus on Google. Like most of the big search engines, Google is crawler-based. It uses a special form of software—often called a spider—that, quite literally, crawls the web. The software looks at the content of a web page and then analyzes whether that page matches a search query.

Google considers more than just the text on a page, however; it also analyzes links to and from that page. It considers the number and quality of sites that link to the page when determining where to rank a site among the hundreds or thousands of others that may also be relevant to a user's query. In addition to links and content, Google also analyzes parts of the structure of a website, including content that users don't see, such as meta tags. A meta tag is a snippet of HTML code placed on a web page describing the content of the site.

Placement in search engine rankings is not for sale; your site lands wherever it lands because of its content, links and keywords. Keywords are what users enter into a search engine when conducting a search; the frequency with which those same keywords are incorporated into the content of your website will help boost your site's placement in response to those queries.

Sound complicated? It actually gets more so: The specific algorithm used to rank the pages returned for any given search query is a highly guarded secret, and one that's liable to change at any given moment.

But having a top search-engine ranking isn't the only way of targeting search-engine users: Google also offers a program called Google AdWords that allows you to bid on keywords. When someone searches for one of those keywords, your ad will appear as a "sponsored link" either on top of or next to the actual search results. Microsoft and Yahoo! both offer similar programs for their search engines, called adCenter and Sponsored Search, respectively.

So while search engines may look simple, in truth they're anything but—especially if you're a business owner trying to figure out why your site isn't appearing on the first, second or even third page of results. After all, placing near the top of Google's—or Yahoo!'s or Windows Live's—search results could increase your site traffic and potentially your business many times over.

That's where search engine marketing and search engine optimization come in. Historically (and yes, this practice has been around long enough to have a history), SEO has been considered the process of optimizing the content of a website, including its use of keywords, in order to organically improve its placement in search engine results.

"We've had SEO almost as long as we've had search engines," says Danny Sullivan, an analyst who studies the search industry. "Think back to the mid 1990s, and you'll recall the services offering to submit sites to various search engines. That was rudimentary SEO."

With the arrival and sky-rocketing popularity of Google AdWords in the early part of this decade, many SEO firms morphed into SEM businesses. Rather than focusing solely on growing traffic organically, these SEM companies began using a variety of practices—including pay-per-click ad programs like AdWords and adCenter—to increase traffic to their client's websites.

Most SEM firms offer SEO services as well; SEM is typically considered a catch-all term for a variety of marketing practices used to increase traffic to a site, while SEO is just one of the ways to do that. Note that some companies use the term SEM to refer only to the for-pay practices, rather than as an umbrella term that encompasses both the paid and organic means of growing traffic. Doing this is not incorrect; it's simply a more narrow use of the term and one that may be easier for your customers to understand. And helping your customers understand your business—and why they need it—is one of the biggest hurdles a search engine marketer may face.

New Media Service

The term "new media" is another internet buzzword that is often overused and can be hard to define. Wikipedia—the online user-generated encyclopedia that many consider a new media service itself—defines it as "the marriage of mediated communications technologies with digital computers."

Say what?

Wikipedia also explains: "New media is the convergence between the history of two separate technologies: media and computing…. New media can be defined not only as things you can see, such as graphics, moving images, shapes, texts and such but also things that cannot be seen such as a Wi-Fi connection."

Wacky for Wikipedia

If you're searching the web for information on a specific topic, you're likely to come across results from Wikipedia. Wikipedia, whose name is a blend of the terms "wiki" (a user-editable, collaborative website) and "encyclopedia," is one of the largest reference sources on the web. The service was launched in 2001; since then, it has amassed more than 9 million articles (of which more than 2 million are in English, according to Wikipedia's own statistics) on a variety of topics. Wondering who coined the phrase "Where's the Beef?" Type it into Wikipedia, and you can find out. Looking for a timeline of Chilean history? You'll find that information, too.

But beware, the information isn't always accurate because Wikipedia is created by the very users who read it. Some users may make mistakes when posting information, while others may intentionally post erroneous information as a form of web vandalism or "spin" an entry as a form of underhanded public relations. Despite this, Wikipedia is both an excellent source of information as well as a shining example of the sheer power of user interaction online. That's something to consider when designing your web service.

We don't use the term to confuse you or to overgeneralize. Instead we use it to point out the wide range of opportunities available online. A new media service could be a video-sharing site like YouTube. It could a streaming-music service like Jango or a personal finance service like Mint. It also could be a mashup application that allows users to aggregate and manipulate various forms of web content, like Yahoo Pipes. It could be a "social browser" like Flock. Or an online game—and embeddable Facebook application—like Scrabulous.

A new media service could be almost anything; you just need to come up with the idea. Do you have an idea for a new way people could be viewing their favorite websites? Or an idea for sharing video content online (legally, of course)? You dream up the service, and we'll provide you with the basics for getting the idea out of your head and into the world.

Starting a new media service can be challenging and inherently risky. In many ways, starting a new media service is reminiscent of launching a dotcom startup in the bubble days we told you about earlier: You're often navigating new and unfamiliar ground, trying to convince people to do something they've done

Stat Fact
Online video is hot. Need proof? According to comScore Video Metrix, in just one recent month, 10 billion online videos were viewed.

their whole lives, like listening to music or viewing their photos, in a whole new way. So you'll need to be able to sell your idea to the public and to investors who may be wary of putting money into another dotcom failure.

But creating a new media service can also be financially rewarding—if you find the right idea and the right way to execute it. Remember when we told you that Google paid $1.65 billion (yes, billion) for YouTube? You likely won't sell your company for that much, but it shows you just how much money is available in this market. Even a small fraction of that would be enough to satisfy most entrepreneurs.

Blogging Business

At first glance, blogs may not seem to have very much in common with new media sites like YouTube and MySpace. Blogs, after all, are typically text-heavy websites, with little in the way of multimedia bells and whistles. But blogs allow almost anyone to have a voice on the web, and they allow authors to interact with their readers. This type of interaction is a hallmark of today's web.

Blogging may seem like little more than a hobby. But we're here to tell you that, yes, you can make money from your blog. That may explain why blogging is booming.

Before we can tackle the business of making money from a blog, we should define the scope of blogs as best we can. The term "blog" comes from the phrase "web log," which was used for a short time to describe websites that published a running archive of dated entries. "Web log" quickly mushed into one word, "weblog," and in turn, morphed into "blog," which has been with us ever since. The word "blog," as a noun, can describe a regularly updated website with dated posts. The word can also be used as a verb, as in "to blog," meaning to submit posts to a website. People who run blogs are known as "bloggers," and all the internet's blogs are collectively referred to as the "blogosphere."

The basic anatomy of a blog is nothing more than a website with dated entries. This encompasses everything from online daily journals to up-to-the minute news sites and more. With the recent emergence of photo blogs, video blogs and comic-strip blogs, the definition of blog is expanding every day.

A blog serves no single purpose. The motivations for starting a blog are as varied as the people who start them. Some people use their blogs to filter the media bombardment that we receive every day via the internet, TV, radio and print media. By rooting through the media din and selecting the most relevant and insightful stories, bloggers can provide a valuable service.

Other people use their blogs to inform like-minded hobbyists about a particular industry. For example, a great number of blogs are about the internet—how to build sites, what technologies to try and what coming trends to watch. These bloggers alert their audience to exciting news by keeping a constant finger on the pulse of a particular pastime and, in that way, provide another valuable service. Bloggers even publish their blogs with the simple intention of making people laugh. Plenty of bloggers post cartoons, funny pictures, charming stories and many other things that they, and their readers, find enjoyable. This, too, is a valuable service. Even big companies such as Google and Microsoft are trying to put on a friendly face by publishing blogs of their own. For little investment, these companies gain the benefits of this intimate and direct medium through which to communicate with their customers.

Future of the Industry

Unlike the failed Pets.com, these four services are not retail businesses—and that's potentially a very good thing since, as the BLS reports, over the 2006-2016 period, goods-producing industries will see overall job loss.

And there are still lessons to be learned from the example of Pets.com. The first one is that while size does matter, it's not everything. Turning a profit is more important than growing on a grand scale. Secondly, you need a firm business plan. Your business may be virtual, but your ideas and your plans to execute them must be put on paper. We'll walk you through that process in Chapter 6.

You'll also need to specialize. The World Wide Web may be endless, but it's no longer the Wild West. Much of the territory that's out there has already been claimed. That doesn't mean there isn't any room for newcomers, but if you want to make your mark, you need a reason to exist. That reason is your specialty; if you specialize, you can become the expert in that niche. In any of these four businesses we're telling you about, you can—and should—specialize. That's the wave of the future.

Web
Design

We have good news and bad news about the web design market. The good news? There's a huge demand for talented, dedicated web developers and designers. Most web designers we talked to say they—and most of their colleagues—continually have more business than they can handle. Sounds great, right?

Well, here's the bad news: This is not a get-rich-quick indus-

▲

stry; some insiders say it's not even a get-rich-at-all kind of industry. You're likely to find yourself making less money than you potentially could by putting your skills to work as a webmaster or a web developer for a big company. Hmmm…sounds less promising, right? Not necessarily: If you're the right kind of person, opening a web design firm can be rewarding, both personally and—eventually—financially.

Is This the Business for You?

Just who is the right kind of person? First off, you need experience building and/or designing websites. Many people use the terms "web designer" and "web developer" interchangeably, but they're not technically the same thing.

"At the most basic level, a web designer handles the graphics, the look and feel of the website, while a developer handles the things you don't see—the HTML, the scripts and the coding," notes James Paden, a web developer from Indianapolis and owner of the *Xemion Web Designer Directory* (xemion.com).

If you have no experience in design or development, you have some learning to do. You should have at least one, and perhaps both, of these skills if you're thinking of starting a web design business. If you plan on working alone—and many web designers do—it may be hard to open shop if you're a graphic designer who can't handle any of the development work and vice versa.

It's possible to find success if you aren't an expert in both these fields, however. Designers who are experts with Photoshop but don't know HTML can either outsource the actual development work or decide to partner with an experienced developer. The same goes for a savvy developer who can't handle the design aspect. You either need to outsource some work to a reliable freelancer, or you need to find a partner.

(Note: We use the term web design company throughout this book because it's the most common label. Keep in mind that we're not referring to a company that handles design only; we are talking about a company that both designs and builds websites.)

Perhaps even more important, you must have a sense of autonomy and a desire to be your own boss, says Pat Patterson, an independent web developer in the Boston area. You need a desire to succeed in a very crowded market.

State of the Market

In the introduction to this book, we told you that it's just about impossible to count how many web design firms exist today. While this is partly due to the fact that there's no one organization that keeps track of these companies, it's also because many of them close up shop as quickly as new ones open. So while that Google search for "web

Smart Tip

Take advantage of all the online resources at your disposal. Web designer directories do more than simply list available web designers; they also offer blogs and forums where you can trade knowledge with other designers and expand your professional network.

design firm" may yield more than 43 million results, it's likely that many of these companies are no longer in business.

"This is an industry with a low barrier to entry. Anyone can throw up a website and call themselves a web designer," says Paden.

Many of those people realize they don't have what it takes to keep their business afloat and quickly abandon ship. "Often, as a professional, I encounter people who come to me and say they're not happy with the site that their web designer built for them, and they've realized that the company has gone out of business," says Paden. "Many of my projects are for clients who have come to me from someone else. Sometimes it's a kid out of high school or college who can design sites but doesn't know how to manage clients or run a business."

Most web design businesses are set up in one of three ways: individuals (freelancers) who work part time; individuals (freelancers or independent contractors) who work full time on their own; or larger companies with several employees. Let's talk about each of these structures a bit more.

- **Part-time freelancers:** These are people who typically work in a web design- or development-related field and take on additional design projects on the side. This can be a great way to start out in web design or to make additional income.

  I never had the desire to work for myself full time," says Nick Giordano, a part-time web designer in the Boston area. "There's a lot of risk inherent in that; I was always fearful there would be a lull in income."

  Working part time allows you to collect the salary and benefits that come with your full-time job while taking on projects you enjoy on the side. "I can pick and choose the work I do," says Patterson. It can also mean a very busy schedule, so you may not have time to take on all the projects you'd like. Your first commitment is to your full-time job; any part-time projects must be tackled when your free time allows. You don't want to take on projects that you can't handle in a timely and

Beware!

As a web designer, you aren't just competing with other established web design firms: You're also competing with anyone who decides to call themselves a web designer. You may find yourself having to justify your rates to new clients who can find less reputable designers charging next to nothing, but remember that your professional services are worth the price you charge.

Using The "F" Word

The day is here: It's time to go into business for yourself. You tell a colleague that you're going to be a "freelance web designer," and you see a look of concern cross her face.

"Never call yourself a freelancer," she whispers. "It's the kiss of death."

Why?

"It can make you sound like a slacker," writes Nick Cernis on his site Put Things Off (http://putthingsoff.com), a blog that provides advice to freelancers. "Try approaching your bank manager for a loan as a 'Freelance Photographer.' Then try somewhere else after dropping the 'Freelance' from your title. You'll be amazed at the difference it can often have," he writes.

Tony D. Clark agrees that freelancers suffer from an image problem: In his Success From the Nest blog, which provides tips for work-from-home entrepreneurs, he once wrote about the time he heard someone say "freelancing is for suckers."

Most freelancers, Clark realized, make just enough money to keep themselves afloat; they are, he writes, just treading water. The key to making more money—and running a more successful business—is to move up in what he calls the hierarchy of the self-employed.

Clark's chart (below) is based on psychologist Abraham Maslow's hierarchy of needs, a study in the factors that motivate most people throughout their lives. Clark applies this same principal to homebased entrepreneurs and the ways you can move through the various levels of self-employment.

You don't have to call yourself a freelancer; you can simply call yourself a web designer or an independent contractor. What really matters is how you handle yourself. You build your reputation and your image through the work you do, not through the label you give yourself.

Self-Employment Hierarchy

responsible manner, so you may be forced to decline projects offered to you.

- **Full-time freelancers/independent contractors:** Typically, full-time freelancers or independent contractors work alone, though this isn't always the case. In most cases, a full-time freelancer running his own company will handle all aspects of

> ## Beware!
> If you have a full-time job but are interested in taking on part-time web design projects, you should check with your employer first. Make sure that doing so is allowed according to the terms of your employment.

designing and developing websites for his clients. Still, some may, as we mentioned earlier, partner with other freelancers who have complementary skills or subcontract extra work.

Working as a full-time freelancer offers some obvious benefits: You can—to a certain extent—make your own schedule, you can work in your pajamas if you choose, and you can take on the clients and projects you want. However, you also

Go Virtual

Here's an idea for a working arrangement that just might combine the best of both worlds: It will let you work from your home, no matter where that is, while still being a part of a larger working team. Form a virtual, collective web design firm.

You can recruit a group of web designers and developers—often people with complementary skill sets and schedules—and work together in a collective arrangement. You and your partners need only be connected to each other and to your clients via the internet.

This type of arrangement will allow you to take on bigger clients and have more flexibility in the kinds of projects you handle. It also will allow you to take vacations without worrying that no one is manning the business.

There are drawbacks, however. Even though you won't be interacting with your co-workers on a daily basis, you may still be subject to "office" politics—the very same politics you wanted to leave behind. And depending on the specifics of your arrangement, you may lose some of the control you would have if you were running the business for yourself.

Should you decide the advantages outweigh the negatives, you'll still want to proceed with caution. Set up the business with as much care and attention as you would any business agreement. Taking the time to do so early on will help you avoid problems later down the road.

▲

assume the risk inherent in foregoing the security of working for someone else: You need to make sure you're earning enough money to make a living, and you need to handle all aspects of the business (including the boring ones) yourself.

- **Web design companies:** These are larger firms with several employees. Some employees may be strictly designers, while others may be coders who handle the back-end work. A web design company may have once been an establishment run by a freelancer that grew to a larger size. Forming this type of company has benefits: You can take on bigger—and better paying—projects, and you can hand off tasks you don't enjoy (like invoicing clients) to other employees. But you may also find yourself back in the type of corporate culture you hoped to escape when you went into business for yourself. You may also find yourself mired in tasks that have more to do with managing employees, making sales and operating a growing business than the actual design and development of websites.

No one structure is right for everyone, and many web design businesses will evolve through all three stages described above.

Competition

The services you decide to offer go a long way in distinguishing your company from your competition, but they also bring in new competition. If you're a freelancer who offers SEO on top of web design, for example, you may find yourself competing with larger firms who offer the same services. This kind of competition with established professionals isn't the only kind you'll face, however. You also have to compete with anyone who decides to call themselves a web designer—perhaps even that high school kid down the street.

The internet has created a huge market for web designers, and it's given them an opportunity to reach new clients without taking geography into account. Many designers, even those who work part time, can take on clients from around the country or even around the globe. This is an incredible boon for talented, hard-working professionals. The number of potential clients they could reach grows exponentially when geography is removed as a limitation.

However, it also gives those same opportunities to less professional companies. We told you that anyone can throw up a website and call themselves a web designer. These websites, many of which are incredibly impressive looking, may lead clients into believing that these companies are large, established firms that can handle their project. In reality, though, the site—and the business behind it—is run by a 16-year-old who has excellent computer skills. His business skills, however, may be less than impressive.

These are people who are not necessarily ill-intentioned; they may have taken on more clients than they could handle or started a business before they were ready. Whatever their reason, they may have burned their clients by taking money and not

Think Outside the Web

If you think your website design company is limited to offering only web design? Think again. If you're looking to attract more clients, consider adding more services to your roster. Nick Giordano, for example, says that his self-named, part-time Boston business offers not only basic site design but also other design-related projects. He will handle print design projects, such as creating logos, either in addition to web design projects or on their own.

Some freelancers and larger firms add web-based features, like search engine optimization (SEO), to their list of services. All web designers should aim to create sites that can easily be crawled by search engines, but some companies go beyond this, adding specific SEO and search engine marketing services. (For more information on exactly what these services are, read Chapter 3.) Some will host sites for their clients, while others will simply recommend third-party hosting companies.

In the end, what you offer is really up to you. "You have to decide what your skill set is," says James Paden, the web developer from Indianapolis, "and from there, figure out what you can offer to your clients."

completing the job or delivering subpar results. In some cases, they may have gone out of business altogether.

That means that you, as a hard-working professional, have to win back their trust. You're competing with the ghost of bad companies that mistreated their clients. You also have to do this while defending the rate you charge. You may have to convince your clients that your services are worth $75, $100, even $150 an hour when a local student is charging $10 an hour.

One of the best ways to do this is to establish your reputation in the field. We'll talk more about this in Chapter 13, but you'll want to network within the industry, become a thought leader, and write blog posts and other articles to demonstrate your expertise. You'll also want to continue to refine your skills and learn as much about new technologies and standards in the continually evolving field of web design.

A Day in the Life

As a web designer, your average day will be determined by how your business is structured. A part-time freelancer will spend much of his time at his full-time job, working on his web design projects at night or on weekends. The founder of a larger web design company will find his tasks determined by the number of employees he takes on. For the purposes of this book, we'll assume you're starting as a full-time freelancer. What can you expect on your average day? In short, a bit of everything.

You have the ability to set your own hours. "You might sleep in until 11 and stay up working until 2 a.m.," Paden says. This was his schedule when he first started out as an independent web designer. As more clients came in, he realized he needed to be more available to answer the phone during typical business hours, so he began doing more of his work during the day. Some freelancers handle all their interactions with clients via e-mail, so they can work whenever and wherever they choose, but you're likely to find that at least some of your clients would like to speak on the phone.

Once you're working on web design projects for clients, you can expect them to take anywhere from a few days to several months to complete, depending on their size. One day could be spent working on a project for just one client or on projects for several clients. A larger web design company is more likely to handle bigger projects that may last for months.

In addition to the actual work of designing and building websites, part of each day will likely be spent on basic business tasks. You'll need to prepare and send out invoices, work on advertising and marketing your business, peruse industry websites and blogs to stay current, and post to your own blog to demonstrate your expertise. You also need to handle queries from current clients; Paden says he spends less time marketing his business now that he gets more referrals and repeat business, but he also fields far more customer support requests. "I get a lot of clients calling asking me to move an image or update a page," he says. "If I get five hours of billable work in, it's a good day."

Getting Started

We already mentioned that you need a good deal of experience designing websites if you're interested in starting your own web design company. You need to demonstrate both your skills and your style to potential clients through a portfolio of your work. Of course, even if you've worked as a webmaster or a web developer in-house at a larger company, you may not have built a portfolio—you have the experience you need to build sites but not the materials you need to show off your skills.

That's why the first thing any aspiring web designer needs to do is to build his portfolio. A great way to do this is to offer your services for free. "You should start by designing sites for your friends, for nonprofits, for yourself," Paden says. "You should give your work away until you're ready to charge for it." How do you know when you're ready? "Typically, if you're not sure if you're good enough, then you're not good enough," he says.

You can get certified in certain skills, like graphic design or web design, but these certifications alone won't be enough to sell your services. "It's great to go to school, but you need actual results to show to someone," says Giordano, who is certified in both web and graphic design.

Paden recommends taking the time to study the work of leading web designers: "Look at CSS galleries, Flash galleries, collections of pages online that people have decided are good pages. See what you like about them; compare your work to their work."

You also want to create—and maintain—a website that reflects your style and displays your portfolio, Giordano recommends. This is one of the most important ways you can showcase your skills. After all, would you hire a web designer with a poorly designed website?

Another way to establish your reputation—and to gain paying clients—is to specialize, whether that means offering sites geared toward a specific industry, like accountants or lawyers; using Flash; or offering e-commerce features. This gives you the ability to bill yourself as an expert, Paden says. It also gives you the opportunity to work on the aspects of web design you enjoy most. "That's the advantage of being a freelancer," he says, "You pick what you do."

Equipment

To run a web design firm, you're obviously going to need a computer; it doesn't have to be a top-of-the-line system, but it should be reasonably powerful. You should spring for a system with a good-sized hard drive (minimum 250GB to 320GB, but you can opt for a drive up to 750GB or even 1TB) and plenty of memory (1GB is the bare minimum; anywhere from 2GB to 4GB is optimal) to run the graphics programs you'll need. Keep in mind that graphics programs can hog your PC's resources, so springing for a system with plenty of memory and a powerful processor can save you time and money down the road. You can use either an Apple or a Windows-based PC; many designers use both, which can be beneficial when checking if a newly built site is rendering correctly in different browsers.

No matter what type of computer you use, you may benefit from a large monitor—or perhaps two monitors. A spacious display (22 inches or bigger) allows you to view multiple program windows at once without having to toggle back and forth between them. If you already own one monitor and want to expand your screen real estate, you can do so by adding a second monitor. You connect

Dollar Stretcher

An online backup service can provide an easy and less-expensive alternative to purchasing a backup hard drive. You'll need to select a reliable and secure service—and you should make sure you know what will happen to your data should the company go out of business.

both to your PC, and then set your operating system to spread your desktop across the two displays. This, too, allows you to work with many windows open at once and can be useful when you need to copy information from one application to another.

A back-up hard drive can save you—and your business—should anything go wrong with your computer. It can also help you retrieve information that your client may lose. You'll want to schedule regular backups to ensure your informa-

Dollar Stretcher

Consider buying a packaged suite of software instead of individual applications. Adobe's Creative Suite 3 Web Premium includes the latest versions of Dreamweaver, Flash Professional, Photoshop Extended, Illustrator, Fireworks, Acrobat Professional and Contribute for $1,599.

tion—from current works in progress to your client database—is saved.

Not all web design companies host their clients' sites, but if you do, you'll likely need your own server. Many web design firms recommend third-party hosting companies instead of hosting sites themselves.

While the hardware requirements for your web design company are relatively inexpensive, we can't say the same about the software.

Dollar Stretcher

Consider free open-source alternatives when looking for software. You may be able to find applications that handle design or vector art, or provide stock imagery for free.

Photoshop is a good example. This Adobe application is a key tool; it allows you to manipulate images and create graphics—like buttons—for your sites. The basic version of Photoshop Creative Suite 3 starts at $649; the Creative Suite 3 Extended version (which adds tools for working with video and other multimedia files) lists for $999.

You'll also need Adobe Dreamweaver ($399), which is used to build the actual framework behind the page; Adobe Flash ($699), which allows you to create rich media and interactive web content; and Adobe Illustrator ($599), a drawing application for creating web artwork and graphics.

Your software needs aren't limited to Adobe's applications only. Should you offer any specialized services—like SEO—you'll require the often-pricey applications needed to provide them. You can find more information on those applications in Chapter 3.

Typical Staffing Needs

A freelance web designer, even one who works full time, isn't likely to need any employees. Most are content to work on their own for as long as their business exists.

Some people do better with partners, however—especially when they can bring on partners who provide skills they lack. Others team up when the workload becomes too big to handle.

In the end, whether you hire employees will likely depend on the goals you—and your partners, if any—have set for your company. If you want to grow, you're going to need help—whether that help is a salesperson, a bookkeeper or a web programmer is really up to you.

Money Matters

We told you at the start that this is not a get-rich-quick kind of industry. We even warned you that you may never get rich at all while working as a web designer. Still, you can make a good living as a freelance web designer—and you'll have the lifestyle you want while doing so. And, if you have experience dabbling in web design, it's likely you already have some of the equipment you need to start your own company. That means your startup expenses will be gradual; you don't necessarily need to spend a lot of money all at once.

Startup Costs and Income Potential

To estimate how much money you'll need to start your web design business, we're going to assume you're working out of your home, so we're not adding office rent in to the equation. Here's how much you can expect to spend on some basics. (Note that these estimates will vary based on where you live.)

You can furnish your home office, including a desk, chair, phone and filing cabinets, for about $500. You also can expect to spend about $100 (less if you're frugal) on supplies such as paper, staplers, paper clips, printer ink and such; add another $100 if you need company letterhead and business cards.

Expect to spend $1,500 on a good computer desktop system (a high-end laptop will likely cost more) and about $2,000 on the necessary software if you don't already have what you need. An extra hard drive for backing up your data will run you about $200.

Add in $100 for miscellaneous services (such as registering your domain name, hosting fees for your website, and the cost of installing your office phone line). If you have an attorney review the contracts you plan to use with your clients—we've provided a sample at the end of this chapter you could customize to fit your needs—add another $200.

As you can see in the "Sample Startup Costs" chart on page 23, you can expect to spend about $5,200 to start your web design company. That includes one-time upfront expenses, as well as the first month of the recurring costs, such as your phone and internet access bills. You likely won't need to spend very much on advertising before you launch, and you won't require the services of an accountant. Overall, your

▲

startup costs are quite low—especially when you consider that many web designers will already have much of the necessary equipment. You can estimate your own startup costs on the work sheet on page 24.

With such a low investment, how much can you expect to make? Your income will vary based on your status; part-time freelancers will obviously have less time to devote to their business and therefore the ability to take on fewer clients. As a full-time freelancer, you can likely make at least $30,000 your first year. As you develop your skills—and raise your rates—your income will climb accordingly. Paden estimates that higher-end freelancers can make in the neighborhood of $60,000 per year. Making a six-figure salary as a freelance web designer is a challenge, though it is possible. But most people don't enter this field to become millionaires; they do it because they love it.

Sample Startup Costs

Item	Cost
Office Rent	$0
Computer hardware	$1,700
Computer software	$2,000
Office supplies/equipment	$700
Internet access	$45 per month
Phone service	$45 per month
Advertising	$50
Insurance	$0
Domain name registration	$9
Web hosting	$7 per month
Legal fees	$200
Subtotal	$4,756
Miscellaneous expenses (10 percent of subtotal)	$476
Total Startup Expenses	**$5,232**

Startup Expenses Worksheet

Item	Cost
Office Rent	$
Computer hardware	$
Computer software	$
Office supplies/equipment	$
Internet access	$
Phone service	$
Advertising	$
Insurance	$
Domain name registration	$
Web hosting	$
Legal fees	$
Subtotal	$
Miscellaneous expenses (10 percent of subtotal)	$
Total Startup Expenses	$

Sample Website Design Contract

Client Information:
[Name]

1. Authorization

The above-named Client (hereinafter referred to as "Client") is engaging Gallantry Web Design as an independent contractor for the specific purpose of designing a World Wide Web site, hereinafter referred to as "Web Design Project," to be published on the Client's account on an Internet Service Provider (ISP)/Web Presence Provider (WPP) computer, hereinafter referred to as "Hosting Service," or provided on CD at the Client's option. The Client hereby authorizes Gallantry Web Design to access this account and authorizes the Hosting Service to provide Gallantry Web Design and its designer, Rebecca Gallant, with "full access" to the Client's account and any other programs needed for this Web Design Project that are included as part of the Client's service agreement/level. The Client also authorizes Gallantry Web Design to submit the completed Web Design Project to major web search engines.

2. Development

This Web Design Project will be developed using Macromedia Dreamweaver.

> • *Compatibility:* Designing a website to fully work in multiple browsers (and browser versions) can require considerable, extra effort. It could also involve creating multiple versions of code/pages. Gallantry Web Design represents and warrants that the website we design for you will work in:
>
>> Microsoft Internet Explorer
>> Netscape Navigator/Communicator
>> Mozilla Firefox

While Gallantry Web Design will make reasonable efforts to design a fully functional website, Gallantry Web Design's warranty does not cover AOL, text-based browsers or requested special effects that we have advised you against.

> • *For People With Disabilities:* Gallantry Web Design's standard is to meet at least half the currently recommended guidelines for website development. Without sacrificing quality and design, we try to

ensure that the content and functions we build into our websites are available to all visitors.

3. Assignment of Web Design Project

Gallantry Web Design reserves the right, and you hereby agree, to assign subcontractors to this Web Design Project to insure that the terms of this agreement are met, as well as on-time completion.

4. Copyrights and Trademarks

The Client unconditionally guarantees that any elements of text, graphics, photos, designs, trademarks or other artwork furnished to Rebecca Gallant and/or Gallantry Web Design for inclusion in the Web Design Project are owned by the Client, or that the Client has permission from the rightful owner to use each of these elements, and will hold harmless, protect, indemnify and defend Rebecca Gallant and Gallantry Web Design and its subcontractors from any liability (including attorney's fees and court costs), including any claim or suit, threatened or actual, arising from the use of such elements furnished by the Client.

5. Website Maintenance

This agreement allows for minor website maintenance to pages for the lifetime of your website at no charge, up to an average of one half hour per regular web page, including updating links and making minor changes to a sentence or paragraph. It does not include replacing nearly all the text from a page with new text, major page reconstruction, new pages, guestbooks, discussion webs, navigation structure changes, attempted updates by Client repairs or Web Design Projects delivered to Client via CD, U.S. mail and e-mail. The period begins on the date the Client's website is available to be published to the Client's hosting service. Major page code and/or graphics changes and additions will be charged at the $50.00/hour rate. (Notice: This rate is subject to change at any time.)

6. Completion Date

Gallantry Web Design and the Client must work together to complete the Web Design Project in a timely manner. We agree to work expeditiously to complete the Web Design Project no later than 30 days after Client has submitted all necessary materials. If the Client does not supply Gallantry Web Design with complete text and graphics content for this Web Design Project within 45 days of the effective date of this agreement, the entire deposit amount of the agreement shall be retained by

Gallantry Web Design as liquidated damages and the contract shall become null and void, at Gallantry Web Design's option, unless the Web Design Project is cancelled in writing by the Client prior to 45 days of the effective date of the agreement.

7. Project Delivery

The final Web Design Project will be published to the Client's hosting service upon receipt of final payment or delivered via CD upon the receipt of full payment. The Client understands that Gallantry Web Design does not provide any hosting services in connection with this Web Design Project. Hosting services require a separate contract with the hosting service of the Client's choice. The Client agrees to select a hosting service, which allows Gallantry Web Design full access to the Client's account via FTP (File Transfer Protocol). The Client will be solely responsible for any and all hosting service charges.

8. Electronic Commerce Laws

The Client agrees that the Client is solely responsible for complying with any laws, taxes and tariffs applicable in any way to the Web Design Project or any other services contemplated herein, and will hold harmless, protect and defend Rebecca Gallant and Gallantry Web Design and its subcontractors from any claim, suit, penalty, tax, fine, penalty or tariff arising from the Client's exercise of internet electronic commerce and/or any failure to comply with any such laws, taxes and tariffs.

9. Web Design Project Copyright

Copyright to the finished Web Design Project produced by Gallantry Web Design will be owned by Rebecca Gallant and/or Gallantry Web Design. The Client will be assigned rights to use the Web Design Project as a website, once final payment under this agreement and any additional charges incurred have been paid. Rights to photos, graphics, source code, work-up files and computer programs specifically are not transferred to the Client, and remain the property of their respective owners.

10. Payments

Payments must be made promptly based on the terms of this Web Design Project. Gallantry Web Design reserves the right to remove any Web Design Project from viewing on the internet until final payment is made. All payments are to be made within 30 days after completion and approval of the Web Design Project by the Client. In the event collection proves necessary, the Client agrees to pay all fees (including all attorney's fees and court costs) incurred by that process. This agreement becomes effective only when signed by Gallantry Web Design. Regardless of the place of signing of this agreement, the Client agrees that for purposes of venue, this agreement was entered into in Rockingham County, New Hampshire, and any dispute will be litigated or arbitrated in Rockingham County, New Hampshire, and the Client hereby consents to the personal jurisdiction of the New Hampshire State Courts. Furthermore, the Client waives any right to or claim of sovereign immunity. Adding of meta tags (description and keywords) and the submission of the Web Design Project to web search engines and updating occur only after the full final payment is made. All payments will be made in U.S. dollars.

11. Payment Schedule

Payment for services provided hereby shall be made in accordance with the conditions contained in this contract and the package price, attached hereto and made a part of this agreement hereof. Notwithstanding any prices listed in literature or on web pages, the Client and Gallantry Web Design agree that the services described in this contract, and the package price, shall be completed for $_____. The Client agrees to pay to Gallantry Web Design an initial, non-refundable deposit of $_____ (normally, 50 percent of the estimated total cost) upon execution of this agreement. Final payment is due within 30 days prior to publication and/or delivery of the Web Design Project. All amounts must be in U.S. dollars.

12. Legal Notice

Notwithstanding anything to the contrary contained in this contract, neither Gallantry Web Design, nor any of its employees or agents, warrants that the functions contained in the Web Design Project will be uninterrupted or error-free. The entire risk as to the quality and performance of the Web Design Project is with the Client. In no event will Rebecca Gallant and/or Gallantry Web Design be liable to the Client or any third party for any damages, including, but not limited to, service interruptions caused by acts of God, the hosting service or any other circumstances beyond our reasonable control, any lost profits, lost savings or other incidental, consequential, punitive or special damages arising out of the operation of or inability to operate this Web Design Project, failure of any service provider, of any telecommunications carrier, of the internet backbone, of any internet servers, your or your site visitors' computer or internet software, even if Gallantry Web Design has been advised of the possibility of such damages.

13. This Agreement

This agreement constitutes the sole agreement between Gallantry Web Design and the Client regarding this Web Design Project. Any additional work not specified in this contract or any other amendment or modification to this contract must be authorized by a written request signed by both Client and Gallantry Web Design. All prices specified in this contract will be honored for six months after both parties sign this contract. Continued services after that time will require a new agreement.

The undersigned hereby agree to the terms, conditions and stipulations of this agreement on behalf of his or her organization or business.

This Agreement constitutes the entire understanding of the parties. Any changes or modifications thereto must be in writing and signed by both parties.

AGREED TO:

Client

(Sign)By_____ Date _____
(Print) Name:
Title:
Address:
Phone:
E-mail:

Gallantry Web Design

By_____ Date _____
Rebecca Gallant
Its Authorized Representative

Source: Rebecca Gallant and Gallantry Web Design

3

Search Engine
Marketing

The buzz surrounding search engine marketing (SEM) can be deafening. This is a hot industry, to be sure, but it's also a crowded one. Still, most industry insiders agree that SEM spending will continue to grow: SEMPO (Search Engine Marketing Professional Organization), a non-profit group that tracks the search engine marketing industry, estimates that spending on SEM will double by 2011, reaching more than $25 billion. With so much money being spent on search marketing, there's more room for newcomers to join this growing field—as long as you go about it the right way.

Is This the Business for You?

It won't surprise you to hear two of the skills that will help you start an SEM firm: experience working with search engines and marketing. While this kind of experience helps, you don't need to be an expert in either field to be successful—at least not at first.

If you're interested in starting an SEM business, you'll need to speak the language of the marketing industry. If you have a background in marketing, you're likely already familiar with the lingo and the buzzwords. But if you don't know the difference between an ad campaign and affiliate marketing, now is the time to learn.

An added bonus to a marketing background is any online experience. If you already understand how websites are built, you've got an advantage. "You don't need to know how to design and build a site from scratch," says Todd Mailcoat, an SEO consultant who writes a blog on SEO at Stuntdubl.com. "Knowing the steps behind it—the project management, the elements of a website, having a basic understanding of servers—is helpful."

A rudimentary (or better) understanding of how search engines work is helpful but isn't a requirement. Search engines constantly tweak and alter the algorithms they use to index websites, so the knowledge you have today may be useless tomorrow. Most experts say they continually strive to understand this process; you'll have to do the same to keep your business successful.

Many people start their own SEM firm after working in-house at a larger agency, so they come with a built-in knowledge of SEM and SEO practices. But running the entire business yourself is a far cry from working for someone else. Now you're responsible for selling your service, writing up proposals and contracts, hiring employees, preparing invoices and collecting payments, and keeping up with all the day-to-day tasks necessary to run your business. Sure, you can (and should) hire help when needed, but you need to keep in mind that running your own SEM business is a big jump from working for someone else. Especially important will be finding—and keeping—clients.

"At the end of the day, a search marketing business is really a consulting business. So that kind of experience—where you're really selling a service—is helpful," notes Robert Cavilla, the founder of UpWord SEM, a Boston-based firm.

Marketing, sales and computer skills will help, but they're likely to be useless unless you have the mindset for a constantly evolving industry. "I think you need an extreme tolerance for information overload. You need to be able to disseminate a whole lot of information and not get overwhelmed," Mailcoat says. "You also need an ambitious drive to learn and a passion for the business. It can be very hard, but it can also be very profitable. It can be very powerful."

But as we've heard before, with great power comes great responsibility. So you have to be ready to handle that kind of responsibility before jumping into this very crowded market.

State of the Market

As we told you in the introduction to this book, the SEM market has evolved dramatically in recent years. SEO morphed into SEM as pay-per-click ad programs like Google AdWords exploded in popularity. Some companies ditched SEO practices—the organic means of growing traffic to a site—in favor of SEM practices focused on expanding traffic using paid search tools.

Stat Fact
Clients spend far more on paid search SEM services than they do on organic SEO services, a recent Search Engine Marketing Organization survey found. More than 87 percent of spending went to paid placement services, while less than 11 percent of all spending went to organic SEO services.

Today, that's no longer the case. "You will find some companies that just do the paid side," says UpWord's Cavilla. "A lot of companies sprouted up with the rise of Google AdWords. Still, you don't see a lot of pure SEO or SEM companies. A couple of years ago, you did, but now most companies offer both."

Mailcoat concurs: "Both [organic and paid methods of increasing traffic] have their merits. But combined, they're even more powerful."

While most companies use a combination of paid and organic methods to increase traffic to a website, the way that those methods are delivered can vary. Many SEM practitioners (both individuals who work on their own as well as companies) use a consulting model for their business. This means they provide advice for their clients on how to optimize their website and then let the client implement the changes. As Mailcoat—who works in a consulting capacity himself—explains: "It's more teaching someone how to fish rather than doing the actual fishing. It's more directional and strategic than hands-on."

Then there's the agency model. There's a fair amount of crossover between

Smart Tip
Just because a company calls itself an "SEO provider," it doesn't mean it offers only pure SEO services. Most firms offer a mixture of SEM and SEO services.

▲

the services that a consultant will provide and those offered by an agency. In general, though, SEM agencies—like Cavilla's Boston-based UpWord—do more of the hands-on work for their clients. Like a consultant, an agency typically will begin its work with an audit of a client's website. From there, a consultant may provide advice and move on, while an SEM agency may implement some of the changes for the client.

> ⚠ **Beware!**
> Even if your clients are accepting liability by inputting your suggested changes, you still need liability insurance. Don't go without it.

That doesn't necessarily mean accessing the client's server and making direct changes to the site, though. "We provide all the recommendations and tell them exactly what they need to do their site and how, but we don't go on the server and make the changes ourselves. By the client actually implementing the changes, they're approving them and also accepting liability if something goes wrong," Cavilla says.

From there, an agency typically establishes an ongoing relationship with its clients, providing reports on a regular basis to determine how well the changes are working. They continue to provide recommendations to reoptimize a site as needed.

Competition

One of the reasons the SEM market is so crowded is because the barrier to entry can be very low. "Anyone with a web design firm or anyone who can design web pages can offer search engine optimization," says Mailcoat. "It's a great thing, amazing. That's what I did. It's wonderful and terrible. It's wonderful if you do it well, but there are no checks and balances. It's also extremely competitive."

Your competition includes more than just honest, established SEM firms. There are less-honest establishments that prey on the ignorance of their clients. They come in, claiming to offer SEO services, often making promises they can't keep, and tarnish the reputation of SEM as a whole. The clients, who may have shelled out thousands of dollars, are frustrated with the lack of results and end up believing that the entire SEM field is a sham.

As a hardworking, honest SEM practitioner, you know this field is not a sham. You provide a very valuable service. But one of the hardest parts of your business may be convincing your clients that your services are necessary and worth the fees you charge.

Networking within the industry and taking advantage of the community's amassed knowledge will help you establish your reputation and that of your company. This is a key step toward growing your honest business and growing the reputation of the SEM industry as a whole.

Join the Club

The SEM industry may be competitive, but that doesn't mean it's an unfriendly business community.

"It's competitive in that the people who are adept at what they do know how valuable their skills and their work are, and they're very protective of that. They've spent a lot of time getting to know each other and the community. The people who know what they're doing are open and trustworthy, but at the same time, they're protective of that community," says Todd Mailcoat, the SEO consultant who blogs on SEM at Stuntdubl.com

You can gain entry to that community, and one of the best ways to start is by perusing the many SEO and SEM message boards and forums online. When visiting these forums, though, you should show respect to their members. "You have to have the right approach coming in," says Mailcoat. "There are all sorts of online forums and communities where people offer advice and information. But you can't expect these people to do your work for you. If you're asking a question to a forum, you should make sure you're asking intelligent questions."

That means you shouldn't head to an online forum before doing any research and ask the members to provide you with all the information you need. And, in general, when posting a question to a forum, you should check to see if your question has already been posed by another member.

Once you've gained experience and knowledge in the industry, you should make sure you pay back the community that helped you out. Answer questions posed by newbies in those same forums you used; remember how you got your start and help someone else get theirs.

A Day in the Life

If you work in the search marketing field, your typical day will vary greatly depending on whether you work as a consultant or own an agency.

As a consultant, "I wake up, get my coffee and call my pajamas my work clothes," Mailcoat says. He says that much of his day consists of administrative tasks, sorting through e-mail and a to-do list that's "three miles long—I know I'll never get through it for the day."

Only about 20 percent of his time is actually spent on consulting work for his clients, Mailcoat says. "It's so learning intensive," he explains. "A lot of the day needs to be spent on experiment and research."

▲

Beware the Black Hats

Not all SEM firms use organic or even paid methods to increase traffic to their clients' websites. Some companies opt for unethical methods; this is called "black hat SEO."

According to Wikipedia, "Black hat SEO attempts to improve rankings in ways that are disapproved of by the search engines or involve deception." Black hat techniques include using text that is somehow hidden from the end user, either because it's placed off the page, placed in small tags, or colored the same as the page's background. Search engines can pick up this text that users can't see. Because the site is presented to users in one version but to search engines in another, it's considered deceptive.

Other black hat techniques include cloaking pages, various methods of buying and selling links, or creating fake "doorway" pages to websites. Some of these techniques used to be considered ethical—or "white hat"—techniques, but may have been abused by some practitioners and are now banned by many search engines.

Many black hat techniques work and many provide quick results, so they can be tempting. But search engines can and do look for sites that are using them and may ban these sites from their results pages. In the end, it's not worth the risk to you or your clients.

When Mailcoat is working on a client project, he's typically conducting site audits. This consists of going through hundreds of variables of a website—from its user interface to its back-end code—to understand how to improve its search engine ranking. Most of his interaction with clients is done over the phone and through e-mail; he doesn't always meet his clients in person.

If you choose to start your business as an SEM agency, your day will differ somewhat. First off, you're less likely to be calling your pajamas your work clothes. You still are likely to spend a significant amount of time online, though, whatever you may be wearing.

"Search engines don't tell you how they work, so you have to figure it out," Cavilla notes. One way to do this is to leverage the knowledge of the SEM community that we mentioned earlier. You'll spend time reading and posting to search engine blogs and forums to learn new tips and tricks and stay in touch with the community.

One thing both consultants and agencies need is new business, and finding new clients can be one of the most difficult tasks you face. "So many people—including web designers—claim to do SEO and SEM. They may know a little bit, but you can

Sample SEO Contract

This is a simplified agreement, generally suitable for small businesses only. It's reprinted courtesy of McAnerin Networks. Visit their website (mcanerin.com/EN/legal) to find a more in-depth SEO contract that you may find useful.

Date: XXXXX

SEO Agreement

YYY (The SEO) and XXX (The CLIENT) hereby agree to the following search engine optimization contract.

The SEO will provide search engine optimization and related services for the website owned by the CLIENT, *www.xxxx.com.*

In exchange, the CLIENT will pay the SEO and provide related necessary assurances as agreed below.

Details

The Parties agree to the SEO services outlined in the SEO Proposal sent by the SEO on [Date], incorporated here by reference, with the following repeated here for clarity:

(a) $XXX Initial Deposit

(b) $1,XXX Payment upon presentation of the Final Report

(c) The CLIENT will pay for costs and disbursements such as submission fees. All such costs and disbursements must be approved in advance by both the CLIENT and the SEO.

(d) Neither Party shall have the right of set-off.

(e) There shall be a $50/month late penalty for fees owed.

The CLIENT will provide the access and permissions necessary to perform the work agreed on, and further agrees to not change or alter the content or coding provided by the SEO during the contract period without the SEO's prior knowledge and permission.

The CLIENT warrants that all materials, such as logos and content, are owned by the CLIENT, and there are no copyright or legal issues that may affect the SEO during the course of its work. The CLIENT agrees that all content created and provided by the SEO are copyrighted by the SEO until the final payment for services has been made in accordance with the contract, at which time it reverts automatically and irrevocably to the ownership of the CLIENT. The Parties are independent, experienced, honest businesspeople and will settle issues wherever possible in an amicable manner in accordance with this, resorting to discussion and arbitration rather than litigation whenever there is a problem. This agreement falls under the laws of the State of XXX, USA.

Signed this X day of XXX, 2XXX,

▲

Fun Fact

The term "search engine optimization" was first used in 1997. Its first known use was in a spam e-mail message sent to advertise the services of a new SEO firm.

offer better services. Your potential clients may not understand search marketing. If you're working with a larger company, they may think their web designer is handling SEM," Cavilla says.

This means you have to work hard to sell your services. Keep in mind that in doing so, you may be trying to sell to a director of marketing who knows nothing about search engines. Or you could be meeting with the IT director of a company who knows nothing about marketing. You need to be able to speak both languages and sell to the proper audience. If you can't, you need to partner with someone who can.

Other daily tasks will include managing client accounts and running campaigns. This can mean doing keyword research one day and checking site analytics the next. One day may involve very technical work, while the next will involve communicating with clients and marketing your company. So you—or your partners—need to be able to handle these tasks and more.

You'll also want to establish your reputation as an industry and thought leader, Cavilla says. In the early days, you may turn to forums for advice, but as you gain experience and knowledge, you should become the person answering those same requests. You'll also want to write articles and blog posts that will get your name out to the community.

Getting Started

Before you can establish yourself in the community, you need to gain some experience. It can be a challenge to get experience without clients, but—of course—it can be difficult to land clients when you don't have any experience. Luckily, there are a couple of ways around this dilemma.

The first is to create your own sites and use them to test your SEO and SEM skills. You can use these sites as case studies to show prospective clients who will want to see results. Another option is pro-bono work; take on a few clients for free, and then use these results to market yourself to potential paying customers. Don't think of it as a waste of your time—think of it as an investment in your company.

Equipment

The hardware necessary to get your SEM business up and running is minimal: a computer and a phone will suffice. You can work off of a laptop or a desktop PC, whichever your prefer, and can operate with a landline or a cell phone—again, it's a

School Days?

When you're first starting out, you may consider enrolling in an SEO or SEM certification program. Many organizations claim to offer these types of programs, and, at first glance, they may seem like a good way to gain knowledge in this often-confusing industry. Unfortunately, though, many of these programs are shams.

Before you sign up for any sort of class or program, do your research. Look into the company offering the courses. Ask other SEO and SEM practitioners if the courses are worthwhile. Don't hand your money—and your time—over to anyone before you're sure of the course's value.

There are some reputable organizations that offer courses. Search Engine Maketing Professional Organization (SEMPO), for example, offers online courses through its SEMPO Institute (sempoinstitute.com). Google also offers an AdWords Learning Center (google.com/adwords/learningcenter) and an exam that, if you pass it, allows you to become a Qualified Google Advertising Professional. Google's certification can be earned on an individual or company level.

matter of preference. You don't need a server right way; you're not likely to be hosting web pages for anyone. Later on, you may need a server for your own internal use, but it's not necessary up front.

The more essential equipment are the software tools you'll use to run your business. The way that search engines index and rank websites in their search results is constantly changing. That means the tools SEO and SEM practitioners use change frequently, too. One company could sell a tool that allows you to analyze who comes to your website and from where; the next day, Google could offer that tool for free.

What we offer here is a rough outline of software applications and web services that many SEM professionals use. Before making any investments, however, you should research the current state of the industry to make sure these tools are still necessary. Many of these tools are free, but before you pay for any that aren't, you should also find out if any

Dollar Stretcher

Before paying for any SEO or SEM software applications, find out if a free version is available. Many companies offer free applications that work almost as well as their paid counterparts, and the search engines themselves offer many analytics tools for free.

new, free alternatives are available. And keep in mind that, in some cases, you may need to spring for a paid version even when free alternatives are available.

- **Site analytics tools:** A wide variety of free and fee-based tools are available to help you analyze the performance of your clients' websites and keywords. These tools tell you how many people are coming to the site and where they are coming from. Google Analytics (google.com/analytics) is a free, full-featured tool. ClickTracks (clicktracks.com), which analyzes how visitors navigate websites, is available in hosted and downloadable versions, starting at $995. Other analysis tools are available from Omniture, WebPosition and WebTrends. There are many, many more analytics tools available—far too many to list here—that offer a variety of features and services. Before you plunk down any money for a tool, do your research carefully and try to find a free trial to see if it fits your needs.

- **Keyword research tools:** Many of these are freely available on the web; others cost about $50 per month for a subscription. They allow you to research the words ("keywords") that people use when searching, so you can find out which keywords are the most popular for certain categories. WordTracker.com is a paid keyword research tool ($329 per year), as is KeywordDiscovery.com (about $600 per year for the standard version). Google offers a free keyword research tool at google.com/trends, but it's more limited in scope than the paid services.

- **Competitive analysis/research tools:** These allow you to find out what keywords your clients' competitors are using, what kind of traffic they're getting, and what kind of changes they're making to their sites. Alexa (alexa.com) and Compete.com will show you trends in site traffic. Alexa is free; Compete.com offers both free and paid tools. HitWise (hitwise.com) is another research tool but is available to subscribers only and can be pricey: A subscription can run in the tens of thousands of dollars.

- **Link building/analysis tools:** Links help websites earn better rankings, but not all links are equal. Links from sites that are considered well-known and trustworthy in the eyes of the search engines (and in the eyes of most web surfers) carry greater weight. These tools can help you develop better links for your clients. You can use free services, like Google's Directory (google.com/dirhp), to find sites you may want to link to and request links from. Other tools help you analyze the performance of current links. SEOBook.com offers a list of tools— including ones (like the Xenu Link Sleuth) that help you identify broken links and others that help you find out if other sites are still linking to your site—at http://tools.seobook.com/link-tools. Many of these are free.

Many more SEO and SEM tools are available online, including search engine rank checkers, which allow you to monitor how your sites rank according to popular search engines; bid management tools, which help you manage pay-per-click (PPC) campaigns; and tools for targeting local search engines. For information about more

Smart Tip

If you decide to hire a sales-person, remember that he or she must understand your industry. A great salesperson can't sell your service if he doesn't know what he's selling.

SEO/SEM tools, visit Todd Mailcoat's website at stuntdubl.com/tools.

Typical Staffing Needs

SEM consultants may always work alone and never have the need to hire additional help, but SEM agencies are likely to hire employees. You may find that you need administrative or sales help; you may also find that you need employees who can handle the SEM applications themselves. In order to grow and take on more clients, you're likely to need employees who can work directly with those clients.

You'll have to pay those workers well: Entry-level workers typically make between $30,000 and $50,000 per year. Once they have a few years of experience, Cavilla estimates their salary typically rises to about $70,000.

Money Matters

You can make a good living from your SEM company, but just how good? It's time to talk numbers.

Startup Costs and Income Potential

Just as the barrier to entry in the SEM field is low, so too is the cost of entry. If you don't need office space (and you may not right away; we'll discuss this in Chapter 9), your costs are even lower. Expect to spend about $500 on office furniture and equipment for your home office (including a desk, chair, phone and filing cabinets) and then about $200 on basic office supplies like paper, ink, business cards and company letterhead.

You'll need a computer if you don't already have one; expect to spend about $1,000 to $1,500 on a decent desktop or laptop. You'll need to spend about $1,000 on the necessary software applications and then another $200 a month on the subscription-based software tools. Add in another $500 for a printer. You likely won't need a server at startup, but if you do, it will cost about $1,000.

You should have an attorney review your client contracts (see the sample contract on page 37), and you may also need one to set up and formalize your business structure. This can range from $200 to $1,000 or more, depending on the complexity of your documents. A small shop may not need the services of an accountant at startup; if you do, you can expect to spend $2,000 to $5,000 to have your financial statements created or reviewed and your books set up.

Your other costs (which we'll discuss in the section on operating expenses in Chapter 11) include phone service, internet access, business insurance, travel expenses, website hosting and domain name registration, and any advertising you decide to do. Ultimately, you can expect to spend about $7,700 at startup and in the first month of running a single-person SEM shop. You can see a complete breakdown of the estimated startup costs for launching both an individual operation and a two-person agency in the chart

> ### Stat Fact
> The majority of search marketers with zero to three years of experience make between $30,000 and $40,000 per year, according to a recent salary survey conducted by SEMPO. To earn a salary in the mid-to-high $100,000 range, you need about five to seven years of experience.

on page 43. You also can use the work sheet on page 44 to calculate your own startup expenses.

How much can you make? At first, you may find it a struggle to make anything at all—whether you're working as a consultant or setting up an agency. You may find that you spend more time on research and development work, and building websites and testing out SEO and SEM practices on them. You may spend little time on billable projects for clients. You may also spend a lot of time finding clients. Most industry insiders agree that it can be difficult to turn a profit during your first year.

After that, the news gets better. Consultants typically start out charging $40 to $50 an hour, and it goes up from there; experienced, in-demand consultants can charge $500 per hour for their work. Most agencies charge either an hourly fee or a monthly retainer for their SEO services. (We'll discuss how—and how much—to charge for your services in Chapter 10.) An established company may be able to charge a retainer of $3,000 per month, while a startup may only charge $800. For the sake of our calculations, we'll say you're charging $1,000 per month. If you have five clients, you can bring in $60,000 per year, on the organic side alone.

For your SEM services, you'll typically earn a percentage of your clients' "media spend"—anywhere from 5 percent (this is on the low end, and you'd likely only do this when first starting out, if at all) to 15 percent. Clients may spend anywhere from $500 to $200,000 per month. If a client spends $20,000 per month, you could bring in $3,000 per month. That's $36,000 per year for just one client.

And that's only the beginning. Remember when we told you that SEM spending is expected to reach more than $25 billion by 2011? If you get started now, by that time, you should be well on your way to earning big profits.

Sample Startup Costs

Item	Consultancy	Agency
Office rent and utilities	$0	$0
Desktop or laptop computer	$1,500	$2,500
Server and printer	$500	$1,500
Computer software	$1,000	$1,500
SEO/SEM subscription services	$200/month	$400/month
Other supplies/equipment	$700	$1,500
Internet access	$45/month	$100/month
Phone service	$45/month	$100/month
Legal fees	$200	$750
Accounting fees	$0	$3,000
Business insurance	$2,000/year	$4,000/year
Travel	$200/month	$300/month
Advertising	$500	$500
Domain name registration	$9	$9
Web hosting	$84/year	$84/year
Employee salaries	$0	$0*
Subtotal	$6,983	$16,243
Miscellaneous expenses (10 percent of subtotal)	$698	$1,624
Total Costs	**$7,681**	**$17,867**

*You can start up without renting office space or hiring employees, at least initially.

Startup Expenses Worksheet

Item	Estimate
Office rent and utilities	$
Desktop or laptop computer	$
Server and printer	$
Computer software	$
SEO/SEM subscription services	$
Other supplies/equipment	$
Internet access	$
Phone service	$
Legal fees	$
Accounting fees	$
Business insurance	$
Travel	$
Advertising	$
Doman name registration	$
Web hosting	$
Employee salaries	$
Subtotal	$
Miscellaneous expenses (10 percent of subtotal)	$
Total Costs	$

New Media
Service

You're reading this chapter because you've decided that you want to launch a new media service. Excellent!

As we mentioned in the introduction to this book, the new media landscape is wide open; we told you it could be anything from an interactive personal finance site to a service for sharing photos. But let's talk about this in a little more detail.

A new media service can truly be anything you dream up. One way to get your dreams started is to look at the new media services that already exist. Here's a brief list:

- **Social networking sites:** Facebook, MySpace and LinkedIn are the big names in this category, but there are many more—Bebo, Friendster, Meetup.com, Ning, Twitter and Xing, just to name a few.

- **Social bookmarking and news sites:** These allow users to save their favorite web pages or news stories and share them with others. Popular services include del.icio.us, Digg, Furl and StumbleUpon.

- **Casual gaming:** These are games, available as a download or playable online through the use of Flash or ActiveX, that are not necessarily designed for hard-core gamers. (Think Tetris, not Grand Theft Auto.) Some popular casual games include Scrabulous, Bejeweled, Slingo, and various forms of Sudoko and poker.

- **Media services:** YouTube is the success story in this category, but it's far from the only one. There's also Hulu.com, Flickr, Revver and many, many more.

- **Collaboration/productivity services:** Launching a productivity service may not seem as exciting as building the next big gaming site, but there's a market for these sites. Current examples include Basecamp, Plaxo, Socialtext, WebEx Web-Office and more.

- **Web publishing services:** We mentioned Twitter as an example of a social networking service, but it's also a web publishing service. Many sites and services cross over between categories. Other web publishing services, which let you post information online, include Blogger, Tumblr and LiveJournal.

See? We weren't lying when we told you that your new media service really could be anything.

Now that you have an idea, it's time to defend it. What makes you think it's good enough to become the next Facebook or the next MySpace? What's so special about your business that it's going to succeed where hundreds—maybe thousands—of businesses have failed?

We're not trying to discourage you by asking these difficult questions. We're merely trying to prove a point: If you're interested in launching a new media service, these are the types of questions you're going to face. And in the early days of your business, you're likely to face them constantly. So if just reading them was enough to scare you, this might not be the best business for you.

Is This the Business for You?

Starting a new media service is different from starting any of the other services we talk about in this book. First, as we mentioned before, the sky's the limit—your new media service can be almost anything you want. Second, the rewards could

Smart Tip

Tip...

One of the best ways to learn about new media services is to join them. Most sites are free, and an account takes only a few minutes to create. While engaging in this fun research task, take notes on what you do and don't like, and how you can improve upon these services.

be much higher—your company could become the next big thing. And third, unlike some of the other net services we talk about in this book, a new media service is hard to run as a one-man shop. So as your dreams and plans grow, so too do the risks—and the expenses. If your dreams are big, chances are your bank account will need to be big, too.

What kind of constitution do you need if you're interested in starting a new media service? "You need a stomach to ride a roller coaster," says Rick Marini, an entrepreneur who co-founded the personality testing site Tickle.com (originally named eMode.com) in 1999. Marini and his partner sold Tickle to Monster.com in 2004 for $100 million, and he is now developing a social media website focused on music called MyRockStar.com.

"On the internet, things move at three times the speed of any other field. New technologies are always coming along, people are always coming and going," Marini says. "You have to understand and embrace risk taking. And you have to be fired up and have passion every day. You have to love what you do."

A stomach made of steel will help; so, too, will any kind of internet experience. Speaking the language will help you get financing, attract employees, and converse with others in the industry. Also helpful is a background in software engineering. If you have the technical acumen

Smart Tip

Tip...

Before you start talking to anyone in the new media industry, take the time to learn the language—especially the buzzwords. And there's no better place to get a handle on internet buzzwords than the internet itself. But don't head to the information superhighway. That's so 1999. Take a quick tour of the blogosphere instead.

to take an idea from your head and actually translate it onto a web page, you start with an advantage.

You don't have to be an engineer to be successful, however; Marini's background was in business when he started Tickle. "You just need to be smart enough to recognize your own limitations," Marini says. "An engineer needs to know if he can go beyond the engineering team. If you lack the ability to talk to people, you may need to partner with someone who has a business or marketing background. You have to know what you're good at and find others who have complementary skills. Recognize your strengths and weaknesses, and fill in the gaps."

State of the Market

Bringing in that added help before you launch can be especially important in today's crowded Web 2.0 market. In the introduction to this book, we mentioned that starting a new media service today can be reminiscent of launching a dotcom startup in the late 1990s. That's only partly true. Last century, the web was an unexplored territory, land that was just beginning to be claimed. If you had an idea for a website, chances were good you could be first on the scene.

Today, chances are better that someone's already had that same idea. It's difficult—often impossible—to be the first on the scene. And you're no longer competing only with other internet startups; you're just as likely to go head-to-head with an "old media" company like *The New York Times*. This isn't necessarily bad news. While the competition is stiff, much of the hard work has already been done for you. Consumers have already embraced the web, so your business model won't come as a surprise. Internet access—especially the kind of high-speed access often required to fully take advantage of a new media service—is more widespread than ever. This means that your potential audience is bigger than ever.

Stat Fact

The number of computer users accessing the internet using a mobile broadband service rose 154 percent between 2006 and 2007, according to a recent survey by comScore Video Metrix. That trend is expected to continue in 2008 and beyond, so remember to think about mobile users when designing your service.

Also on your side is the growth of service-based industries. The Bureau of Labor Statistics predicts that employment in services related to internet publishing and broadcasting will grow 44.1 percent from 2006 to 2016. Internet publishing and broadcasting is a generalization, to be sure, but it's an area where your new media service may very well fall.

Competition

Now that you know the market is primed for the launch of a new media service, it's easy to understand why so many have been launched already. It's now time to talk about the competition your service will face. While a new media service can be almost anything you dream up, it also means that the competition for your business comes from more places than ever before.

Let's say you want to start a service that allows users to share and collaborate on editing their digital photos. You do a quick Google search, and you don't see another site offering all the features you plan on including. Excellent news, right? You don't have any competition.

Ahoy! Web Pirates Persevere

Your web service will face plenty of competition from other legal services, but there's another potential competitor out there, especially if you're interested in a service focused on music or video: illegal file swapping. We're not going to name names, as there's always a good chance that today's illegal services could be gone by the time you read this book. But another—and another and another—service will rise to take its place. These are the services that allow users to download music, TV shows or even full-length new-release feature films for free.

This isn't a reason to cancel your plans for the next great online music service; you only need to consider the success of iTunes to see just how hungry internet users are for appealing, well-designed and, yes, legal alternatives. Before iTunes began offering 99-cent song downloads, internet users had few legal ways to purchase a single song. It was often Napster (in its first incarnation) or nothing. Then Apple came along and revolutionized music downloads with its easy-to-use service. Sure, some people complain vociferously about the strict usage restrictions placed on songs purchased from iTunes, but that hasn't stopped consumers from buying: iTunes has become the largest music retailer in the United States—online or off.

Sure, illegal music and video services still exist, and many of them continue to thrive. But don't let them deter you from your business. Learn from them—and from their mistakes.

Hardly.

You may have found your niche, but your competition is everywhere. What's going to convince people to use your service when they already use Facebook and MySpace to display photos? Competition doesn't just come from services you'd consider your direct competitors—it comes from the established web powerhouses that do a little bit of everything. And, of course, it also comes from specialized services: Why will users bother to sign up for your service—even if it's free—when they already have an account with Flickr and Kodak Gallery? Your competition also comes from the offline world: What's going to convince users to spend their free time using your service when they could be watching TV or reading a magazine?

> **Stat Fact**
> Interested in online video? You're not alone. Almost half (48 percent) of internet users have visited video-sharing sites, according to a recent survey by the Pew Internet & American Life Project.

Despite all this competition, you do have an advantage: You've found your niche. You know the web is crowded with sites and services that all think they can be the next big thing. But finding an untapped (or even just a slightly tapped) market niche is one way to differentiate yourself and rise above the din.

A Day in the Life

In the fast-moving new media world, every day is different. Here are just a few of the things you'll likely do on a day-to-day basis if you're running a new media company.

- **Talking:** If you want your new media company to be successful, you need to be known, and you have to get to know people. So talk! Talk to people in your industry to find out what's going on. Visit social networking sites and blogs to see what's developing in your field. Create your own blog to promote your name.

  But don't just sit in your office and work the phone and your computer—get out from behind your desk. Walk around and talk to your employees. Talk to your sales team, your database administrator, your product people. You should also leave the office to attend relevant industry events and trade shows: To get your name out there, it's important to meet with the people in your field.

- **Reading industry publications:** In the new media world, this doesn't always mean catching up on yesterday's news from *The Wall Street Journal*, though that's important. It means scanning technology news blogs, venture capital blogs, and any blogs or news sites that may pertain to your particular business area.

- **Meeting with investors:** You may be pitching your idea to angel investors, venture capitalists, or even your friends and family if you're looking to raise funding from them.

- **Selling:** Even if you have a sales staff, you should consider yourself the primary salesperson. As the founder of the company, you have the passion and knowledge to sell your service to advertisers. So get out and meet with clients.

- **Whiteboarding:** Marini recommends spending a lot of time in front of a whiteboard with your employees. You can use it to brainstorm, to design your product, and to make sure that everyone in the company can visualize what it is that they're working on. For example, you can use the whiteboard so that everyone can see what certain sections of your website will look like before you put it into actual code.

> **Tip...**
>
> **Smart Tip**
>
> If all your employees are in one place, a whiteboard is a great way to collaborate. But what if your partner is in Boise and you're in Boston? Check out a service like Skrbl.com, which allows you to create a virtual, online whiteboard.

Getting Started

Generating an idea for your new media service is only half the battle. Now it's time to get the actual business end of things up and running.

Equipment

In addition to the basics—telephones, desks, copy machines, fax machines, etc.—that you need to run any business (we'll cover this topic in detail in Chapter 9), getting your new media service up and running will likely require a considerable amount of tech equipment. Luckily, the price of the computers, peripherals and software you'll need has dropped considerably since the dotcom boom days of the late 1990s, so it can be surprisingly affordable to outfit your office.

First, you'll need desktop or laptop computers for everyone on your team. Then, to host your service, you'll need at least one server but possibly an array of servers. You may need a database server and one or several web servers. You likely won't need to store your servers at a location facility to start off; you should be able to house them in your office.

A wide variety of free software is available, which keeps costs down. Free products include the open-source Ruby on Rails (rubyonrails.org) web development framework for creating your web application; PHP (php.net), a general purpose scripting language that's especially suited for web development; and MySQL (mysql.com), an open-source database application.

Your database will be used to store all the information you gather from your users. Even if your site is free, you'll likely need to get some information from your site visitors for customization (a login ID, password and e-mail address) and in order to help sell advertising (demographic data like age and ZIP code). We'll provide more information on this practice in Chapter 10, but for equipment purposes, simply consider it a necessity: You're going to need a database to store that information.

And once your business grows, you'll likely need to migrate to a paid database application, like Oracle. Other reasons for using a paid solution include: if you're offering a secure site and dealing with credit card numbers; if you need hot back-ups (meaning your data is backed up while it's still available to your visitors, so there's no service downtime); and when the value of the data that's being housed becomes critical to the operation of your service. It's also possible that you may simply outgrow some of the free products out there, even though they often scale very well. If you don't know when it's time to upgrade your database software, you need a database administrator—plain and simple.

Typical Staffing Needs

So now you know when you need to hire a database administrator. Who else do you need to hire? Unlike some of the other net services that we talk about in this book, a new media service is difficult to run as a one-person shop.

We already told you that the first thing to do when hiring employees is to look for people who fill your gaps. You'll need to sell your service to investors and advertisers, so you'll need people who can talk. If you can't talk to a crowd, find someone who can. You'll also need at least one programmer or developer—someone who can write the code that will run your service. If you don't speak code, you'll need to find someone who does. According to Marini, you can start your new media company with five to six employees; that should be enough help to get your service up and running.

Money Matters

What's it going to cost you to get that service started? The amount of money you need to launch can vary greatly, depending on how big you're planning to grow. And new media companies have the potential to grow enormously. So let's dream big: Here are some numbers for starting a new media service that will grow to a large size. You can scale these numbers back if your plan is simpler.

Startup Costs and Income Potential

Most experts agree that it'll take about a year before you start seeing revenue from your service. (That's if you're not charging your users, as most services are free. We'll discuss potential sources of revenue in more detail in Chapter 10.) The rough timeline is this: If you're interested in building a true multimedia site/service, you should plan on spending about six months in development. That's the process of taking your idea from a concept in your head, to a plan on paper, to building the back-end code, and then—finally—to seeing your service live on the internet.

From there, you'll likely need to go through a private beta period, where you invite trusted friends, family and associates to test and provide feedback on the service to fix any bugs. You may also go through a public beta, where you open a test version of your service to a wider audience. After one or both beta periods, you may need some time, say a month, to incorporate any necessary fixes and adjustments to your service. Now you're about eight to nine months in, and you're ready to launch your service publicly. But just because your service is live doesn't mean you can expect revenue to come rolling in. Plan on three to four months before you gain any traction in terms of users. Once the users come, so, too, should the revenue, likely from advertisers.

Add all these numbers up, and you should have 12 months to go before you can expect any real money to come through the door. So how much should you have on hand to start?

The five or so employees who you'll need to pay for the first year aren't going to come cheap; your staff is your biggest startup expense—but they're also vital to the success of your business. Later on, in Chapter 12, we'll give you tips for attracting and keeping the best employees. You'll need to start them at a salary of around $40,000 per year. If you're based in a big city like San Francisco, Los Angeles or New York—and there's a good chance you may be after you read our advice on picking a location in Chapter 9—you'll likely have to pay them more than that; a salary of $60,000 per year is more typical in those areas.

And while the price of a server may have dropped since 1999, it's still not free. You can expect to spend about $1,000 per server and a bit less than that on each desktop or laptop you need. You'll likely need to lease office space and purchase or lease the necessary office equipment and supplies. In addition, you'll need to pay for insurance for your business (more on that in Chapter 7), as well as benefits for your employees.

So here come the big numbers. Experts recommend that to launch what should eventually become a very good-sized new media service, you should plan to have about $500,000 on hand for the first year.

Widgets, Widgets Everywhere

We already told you that you need to learn the buzzwords if you're interested in making a go of it on the internet. But we'll let you cut corners and define one of these words for you. Widgets—also known as "gadgets" if you work for Google—are miniature web applications that can be created using HTML, XML, JavaScript or other kinds of web code. They allow users to view information such as news headlines or weather forecasts, view photos, play music and video, play games and much more.

You can create one of these mini web programs and share it via web pages from Google, Apple, Yahoo! and others. It's also possible to convert widgets into Facebook and MySpace applications, which can be shared among users on the wildly popular social networking sites.

You can make money off your widget through advertising, or by using your widget to actually sell products. You may not make millions—or even thousands—of dollars, but you can make money. And creating a widget isn't terribly difficult if you know the basics of web coding. Coming up with an idea (especially a legal idea) for one that will become popular is more difficult. Still, dabbling in widgets can be an excellent way to enter the intimidating new media marketplace.

▲

Now don't close the book in a huff thinking you'll never have that kind of cash. Remember, it can come for a variety of sources—it doesn't all have to come from your checking account. (More info on financing will come in Chapter 8.)

And you don't have to start this big. You may have an idea that will become the next YouTube (and if you launch it after reading this book, feel free to send me my portion of that $1.65 billion payday!). But your idea may be something simpler. If you just want to create a simple Facebook widget to distribute on that social networking site, you can do that with considerably less time and money—less than $1,000 is enough to get you up and running in most cases. You won't need to spend six months in development and pay five employees. It's better to start small than to not start at all. You can see a complete breakdown of the estimated startup costs for launching both a big-time new media service (with seven employees: you, a partner and fire hires) and a simpler service in the chart on page 55. You also can use the work sheet on page 56 to calculate your own startup expenses.

So just how much money can you make from your new media service? The answer, quite literally, is anywhere from a hundred bucks to more than a billion. But to be realistic, it will obviously depend on the size and scope of your service. A Facebook widget earns money by the number of users it attracts; even a popular widget may earn you less than $100 a month to start. Similarly, earning money from a newly launched website is difficult; revenue may top out at a few thousand dollars a month in the early days. But with time and patience (and that hefty slush fund we recommended), it's honestly possible to make a very good living from your new media service. You may not become a millionaire, but if you do your homework right, you should be able to pay the mortgage.

Sample Startup Costs

Item	A Simple Widget	The Next YouTube
Office rent and utilities	$0	$5,000
Desktop or laptop computer	$1,000	$7,000
Servers and printers	$0	$7,500
Computer software	$500	$10,000
Other supplies/equipment	$0	$4,000
Internet access	$45/month	$500/year
Phone service	$45/month	$500/year
Business insurance	$0	$7,000/year
Legal fees	$0	$2,500
Accounting fees	$0	$6,000
Domain name registration	$9	$9
Web hosting	$7/month	$7/month
Employee salaries	$0	$300,000/year
Subtotal	$1,606	$350,016
Miscellaneous expenses (10 percent of subtotal)	$161	$35,001
Total Costs	**$1,767**	**$385,002**

▲

Startup Expenses Worksheet

Item	Estimate
Office rent and utilities	$
Desktop or laptop computer	$
Server and printer	$
Computer software	$
Other supplies/equipment	$
Internet access	$
Phone service	$
Business insurance	$
Legal fees	$
Accounting fees	$
Travel	$
Advertising	$
Doman name registration	$
Web hosting	$
Employee salaries	$
Subtotal	$
Miscellaneous expenses (10 percent of subtotal)	$
Total Costs	$

5

Blogging
Business

All it takes to be a blogger these days is a computer, internet access and an opinion. Thanks to the wide variety of free and easily accessible blogging services, anyone who has something to say now has a platform with which they can deliver their message. Writing a blog doesn't just give you an online soapbox, however; it also offers a viable option for creating your own business. With a little bit of time and effort, you can use your blog as a source of revenue.

▲

Is This the Business for You?

Sure, anyone can be a blogger. Not everyone can be a good blogger, though.

What does it take to be successful? First off, it helps to be a good writer. You don't have to be a professional (though, of course, that can help), and you don't need to have experience or published writing samples. You simply need to be able to write in a manner that's clear and intelligible to your readers. This can be harder than it sounds; if you haven't written anything since that term paper in college, you may want to try your hand at writing something before you set your sights on a career as a blogger. Blogs typically use a more conversational tone than most forms of writing, so you'll want to make sure you're comfortable with that, too.

It also helps to be able to entertain your audience. You can be the most concise writer on the planet, but if you're lulling your audience to sleep, you're not going to succeed. Humor is one way to keep readers entertained; another way is to take a stand.

"People really like a conversational tone applied to things going on in their industry," says Rob May, a blogger who started—and eventually sold—the

Bloggers, Beware!

You have a great new job at a cool new company. You decide to create a blog to detail your experience or to post thoughts and commentary on your industry. Your plan is to publish anonymously, so there's nothing to worry about, right? Think again.

Before you decide to write a blog about your place of employment—even if you're doing so without actually naming the company—you need to consider the risks. And yes, there are risks. Ask Mark Jen, a former Google employee who decided to blog about his experiences at the search engine powerhouse. He was terminated shortly thereafter; the company won't say that his blog was the reason he was let go, but many people have speculated that it was. Heather Armstrong was also fired from her dotcom job in 2002 after blogging about the company. Her site name (and still very popular blog) Dooce.com even spawned a new verb: "dooced," meaning getting fired from a job for blogging about it.

Jen and Armstrong's stories aren't isolated cases: The web is full of tales about fired bloggers. How can you avoid becoming one of them? Before you publish anything, you should research your employer's policy on blogging—if one exists. Many companies don't have a formal policy so you may want to check with your HR department before posting anything online. If you value your job, it's far better to be safe than sorry.

BusinessPundit. com blog. "It also helps if you're willing to take a solid stand on an issue, plant your flag in the ground—even be a little controversial."

Of course, before you take a stand, you should be knowledgeable about the issues and the industry you're discussing. So make sure you do your homework. A good blogger is one who is very interested or immersed in their given topic. You need to be hungry for knowledge and willing to soak up everything that might relate to the subject you're writing about.

If you're a perfectionist, you may find blogging to be a challenge. A blog needs new content constantly. You can't spend weeks—or even days—editing and rewriting individual posts. You need to get content posted and get it posted quickly. That means mistakes will happen, and you'll have to learn to live with that.

State of the Market

Since almost anyone can be a blogger these days, it won't surprise you to hear that the blogosphere is a very crowded place. In fact, it's so crowded, most of the sites and services that attempted to count the number of blogs in cyberspace have given up. Statistics from 2005 and 2006 cite as many as 50 million to 70 million blogs in existence. Since then, most researchers say it's been just about impossible to keep count. Sure, this exponential growth is likely to slow down, but the point is that blogging is big.

Blogging is also big business. It's true that many blogs are written by individuals in their free time and are used as personal diaries or journals, never meant for a wide audience. But more and more individuals and businesses are turning to blogs to make money. A recent study by the Pew Internet & American Life Project found that more than 12 million American adults currently maintain a blog, and nearly 2 million of those bloggers listed making money as one of the reasons they blog.

Most of that money comes from advertising. In the first nine months of 2007, internet advertising revenue totaled $15.2 billion, according to the Interactive Advertising Bureau and PricewaterhouseCoopers LLP. That's an increase of almost 26 percent over the same period in 2006.

Those numbers have gotten the attention of more than just individual bloggers. More and more businesses are turning to blogs for a variety of reasons. Some offline media companies are using blogs as a way to generate more interest in their online content. Other blogs are written by CEOs reaching out to employees, customers or investors, putting a friendly face on a large corporation. Still others are stealthier—written by disguised employees who leak internal company secrets and rumors.

Stat Fact

As many as 175,000 new blogs are created every day, according to blog-tracking company Technorati.

▲

Because there are so many blogs, it can be difficult to establish credibility. But doing so is essential in order to attract—and especially to retain—an audience. The topic you select goes a long way toward building your credibility. We'll discuss choosing a topic in more detail later in this chapter, but you should be certain that your chosen topic is big enough to attract a wide audience but small enough to allow you to realistically be considered an expert in that area.

Competition

When you're writing a blog, you're providing a source of news, commentary and—quite often—entertainment for your audience. So your competition won't only come from other bloggers. Depending on the topic of your blog, you may be competing with newspapers, magazines, TV shows and other leisure activities. If the topic of your blog is celebrities, what's going to draw readers to your site when they could be leafing through the pages of *People* magazine or watching *Entertainment Tonight*? If you're writing about business news, will your readers turn to you—or will they open *The Wall Street Journal*?

Other blogs will certainly compete for your readers' time and attention as well, so you want to make sure your blog can gain traction. This is where that credibility we mentioned earlier will come in. You will do yourself a disservice by entering a topic area that's already chock full of bloggers. Similarly, taking on established field experts can be a prohibitively difficult arrangement. You shouldn't completely disregard your chosen topic if you find that it's crowded or well-covered. In the end, you may have to, but first, consider adjusting your tactics.

If your preferred topic is crowded, readership for that type of blog will be spread too thin across too many blogs, thereby leaving all bloggers with little traffic and little profits. Entering this arena just to publish more of the same may be a mistake. Instead, you should study your competition. Make notes of where people are succeeding and where they are falling behind. Learn from your competitors' mistakes. Then, if you are able to formulate a new approach to the topic or cover it in a new and entertaining manner, it's possible you could draw traffic away from each of the lackluster blogs, create sufficient traffic for your blog, and succeed in bringing cohesion to the once fragmented topic.

A Day in the Life

Publishing a blog can be a full-time endeavor or something you do for added income (and your own enjoyment) in your spare time. That means that a typical day in the life of a blogger can consist of a wide variety of activities. Here are just a few of the things you may find yourself doing on a daily basis.

- **Research:** This doesn't mean going to the library and cracking open an encyclopedia. Your research will depend on the topic of your blog. If you're writing restaurant reviews, for instance, your research will involve looking into new restaurants and going out to eat. If your blog topic is politics, you'll likely be watching speeches and listening to debates. And if you're writing about sports, you'll likely be attending games and watching them on TV.

  Research also consists of gathering information put out there by other experts. Many bloggers link to news articles and other blogs from their own posts, so you should spend time reading this content. Not only will it give you a source of links for your blog, but it will allow you to continually educate yourself in your chosen topic area.

- **Generating content:** After you gather all that information, you need to disseminate it for your readers, so writing is a key task. Generating fresh content for your blog is a must; once you've developed a regular audience, they'll come to your site often, expecting new material.

- **Generating revenue:** We'll cover the specifics of making money in Chapter 10, but if you're interested in profiting from your blog (and if you weren't, you wouldn't be reading this book), you'll need to spend some time on it. This can mean selling advertising space through a program like Google AdSense or working with a network that handles some of the behind-the-scenes sales for you. You may also be preparing and selling merchandise as another means of generating revenue.

- **Dealing with your technology:** You don't have to be technically savvy to publish a blog; today's tools make it easier than ever. But if you want to maintain control over the look and feel of your blog, you may be using an application and a server that can require some maintenance. This isn't likely to be a daily task, but it may come up from time to time, so we're putting it on the list.

▲

- **Watching your traffic grow:** Once your blog is out there in the cyberworld, you—like any proud parent—will want to watch it grow. There are several ways to do this; one is through free services like Google Analytics, which allow you to see who visits your site and how they get there. Other ways to do this will be by reading the comments that users post to your blog and seeing who links to you and why. A great way to build traffic through the use of links is TrackBack, a system that allows a conversation of sorts between two blogs. TrackBack lets one blogger write a blog post about another person's blog; their posting also appears as a comment on the original blog site. Both the blog post and the comment link to one another, allowing readers of each blog to discover the other one.

- **Building a community:** Your readers are key to your blog, so you'll need to spend some time fostering that community. Your blog should attract reader comments, so you'll want to read those comments as a way of understanding what your audience thinks about your work. You should consider the negative feedback as well as the positive, and respond and interact with your readers whenever possible. You'll also—unfortunately—need to deal with comment spam, an increasing problem for bloggers. In addition to online comments, you'll also receive feedback via e-mail, so you'll need to allot some time for reading and responding to messages.

Getting Started

You can't start writing your blog until you've made one very important decision: your topic. You need to decide what you're going to write about before you can do almost anything else. You must have, or develop, a better-than-average familiarity with your chosen topic for readers to take you seriously. Readers won't stick around to read things they already know. You must provide them with the service of your expertise on the subject.

Therefore, you shouldn't choose a topic you know little or nothing about. First of all, learning about your topic as you go will alienate your initial, interested audience and you'll likely develop an early stigma among the people you need most. Second, chances are if you know nothing about it now, you don't have much interest in the subject and your current passion for the topic will wane, leaving you with a blog you can't stand.

Your goal is to grow the audience for your blog, so the topic you select should

Tip...

Smart Tip

Set up a separate e-mail address for your blog that's different from your personal e-mail address. This will help guard your personal address from spam, stalkers and the other security hazards of public e-mail addresses.

have mass appeal of some kind. Begin by thinking about general topics such as sports, technology, fashion or food. Then whittle your idea down to a more specific, yet massively appealing, point. The sports industry, for example, would be too large a topic to cover. People interested in NASCAR won't be interested in your bowling postings. Say basketball is your favorite sport: Cover the NBA. The NBA has millions of fans, and you could produce great traffic by covering the stories that major media pass over.

You also need to choose a blog topic that won't dry up. Public interest is fickle and rarely stays on one topic for very long. So be sure to choose a topic that has not only held the public's interest for a long time but will continue to do so into the future. No one can control public interest, but it can be somewhat predictable. Examine trends in the past, stick to reliable topics, and don't select a subject so esoteric that you limit your own audience.

Blog Boosters

When generating content for your blog, think beyond typical posts. Creating other types of content that your readers may enjoy can help boost traffic. Here are just a few examples of content that can boost your blog.

Are you in the business of reviewing restaurants? Why not create a list of restaurants you're dying to try out and ask your readers for their suggestions, too? Or you could post some of your favorite restaurant recipes or ways to recreate meals from your favorite eateries.

You also might try posting tools and work sheets relevant to your topic area. When operating BusinessPundit.com, for example, founder Rob May created a SWOT analysis tool, which a business can use to analyze its strengths, weaknesses, opportunities and threats. People surfing the web for advice on how to create a SWOT analysis were led to May's blog; this resulted in new readers who weren't necessarily interested in a blog in the first place.

▲

Now that you've decided on your topic, you want to create something of a backlog of content. Many bloggers abandon ship within six to eight weeks of starting a blog, so you want to show your audience that you're going to stick around, notes BusinessPundit.com founder Rob May. One good way to do this is to blog for several weeks before you really begin to reach out to your audience and to other bloggers. Once you've created enough content to prove that your blog will last, you can begin to promote it.

Equipment

The equipment needed to start your blog is minimal, and much of the necessary software is available for free. Obviously, you'll need a desktop or laptop computer with internet access. Really, that's about all you need to buy. If you're interested in posting pictures or videos to your blog (which you might want to consider, depending on your topic), you'll need a digital or video camera, too.

Now you need to select a blogging software platform or service. Here's a basic overview of the blogging software landscape.

There are two main types of blogging platforms: hosted services and server applications. Both perform basically the same task of publishing a blog, but there are significant technological differences between the two. The method you choose will have significant effects on how you run your blog.

Hosted Blogging Service

A hosted blogging service is an entirely web-based service like Gmail. All your interactions with the blogging service, including setting up and posting to your blog, are done through the blogging service's website. There is nothing to download, nothing to install, and you can begin blogging immediately.

Once you register with the service, you're given a URL for your blog. Your blog's address, at least initially, will be some extension of the blogging service's address. Some services allow you to choose this extension, and some assign it to you. Your new blog's address could take the format of any of the following examples:

- **Assigned:** www.genericblogservice.com/12d123dksa9
- **Chosen:** www.genericblogservice.com/cuteK9blog
- **Chosen:** http://cuteK9blog.genericblogservice.com

For casual bloggers, the provided address will usually suffice. If, however, your goal is big traffic (and whose isn't?), you should invest in your own personal domain name and configure it to redirect to the address assigned to you by the blogging service. A domain name registrar such as GoDaddy.com or Enom.com can help you register and redirect a domain. The benefit of this strategy is that you can advertise your own easy-to-remember and more professional domain name, which will automatically redirect your visitors to your blog.

Blogger X

Should you blog using your real name, or should you create a pseudonym? That's a question many bloggers face.

There are some drawbacks to using your real name. First, if you run a blog that feeds off any aspect of your personal life, you run the risk of revealing too much. Second, if you write any sort of highly opinionated or "questionable" material, you may be shooting yourself in the foot when applying for your next job. It's no secret that people often search the internet for the names of prospective employees.

If you aren't publishing highly opinionated or questionable material on your blog and just seek to provide a valuable, thoughtful service for readers, using your real name could be a good move. If you're trying to establish yourself as an expert in your chosen field, a pseudonym could hinder your progress. Media outlets, book publishers and magazine editors looking for potential people to profile or get quotes from are slower to call someone who uses a pseudonym than they are a real person.

Rob May, the blogger behind BusinessPundit.com, kept his real name hidden for his first two years of blogging. "You know your friends and family are reading your blog, and you don't want to offend anyone, so [using your real name] can affect what you write," he says. Eventually, he began posting under his real name for a variety of reasons, including a desire to connect with other bloggers.

If you decide to use a pseudonym, avoid choosing anything inappropriate or offensive. You wouldn't want to alienate potential readers or advertisers. Try to create a memorable pseudonym. Keep it simple, short and witty, if possible.

Blogging services have multiple levels of service, ranging from a basic free service to a more expensive, fully featured service. As your blog outgrows the basic level of service, your fees will increase. The good news is that the top level of service isn't very expensive; services range from $5 to $30 per month for packages that offer enough features to satisfy most bloggers. Hopefully, you'll be able to cover that cost in revenue within a few months of launch.

The disadvantage to hosted blogging services is the limited ability to customize your site. Some services do allow quite a bit, but complete customization isn't possible as you won't have access to much of the code of your website.

Some of the most popular hosted blogging services include Google's Blogger (blogger.com, free), TypePad (typepad.com, $4.95 to $89.95 per month) and WordPress (wordpress.com, free). They vary in the features they offer; some include handy capabilities like posting via e-mail, mobile phone or PDA, which can be convenient for bloggers who don't want to be tied to a desk all day. Before committing to any one service, look at what each one offers to see if it meets your needs. Some services have very limited options when it comes to advertising, for example, so keep that in mind. And remember that new blogging services launch frequently. Be sure to include the latest options when conducting your research.

The main advantages to hosted blogging services are that they're easy to set up, have a relatively low cost of entry, and provide decent features. If you're not known for being handy with server software installations, this may be the best choice for you.

Installed Server Applications

An installed server application is a program that you, the user, install on a server. Available blogging server applications range in size and quality from small hobbyist scripts to large commercial applications. There are free, open-source applications and expensive, proprietary ones. Experiment with the open-source software blogging applications since it won't cost you anything to do so and many of them are better quality than their commercial counterparts.

The main benefit of using an installed application is that you'll enjoy more control over every aspect of running your blog. The server will be under your control (either humming along in your basement or through your web hosting provider), as will be the application, the advertising integration, and the system backups. As you are the one depending on your blog for income, it makes sense that you would want the most control over the service you provide.

One major drawback to this method is that because you have all the control, you also have all the responsibility. If the server goes down, it will be up to you to fix it (unless you're using a web host who can help you with outages). If the blogging application won't load properly, it will be up to you to fix it. And if the advertising doesn't load properly, it will be up to you to make nice with your sponsors…and fix it.

Some of the most widely used and reliably supported blogging applications include:

- **Movable Type (moveabletype.org):** the proprietary blogging application developed by Six Apart, the company that also offers TypePad. It is free for non-commercial use, while other licenses start at $300 per year.
- **LifeType (lifetype.net):** a free, open-source blogging platform that allows multiple blogs with multiple contributors
- **b2evolution (b2evolution.net):** a free, open-source platform that supports multiple contributors and blogs
- **WordPress (wordpress.org):** the free application that was the precursor to the WordPress.com web-based service

Each of these applications comes with extensive instructions on how to install it on a web server and what's necessary to do so. This can be a tricky process, as there are many factors involved. If you find yourself intimidated by the idea of installing your own application, you might want to consider a web-based service. However, if you know how to wrestle an application onto a server, or if you're up for learning the task, an installed server application can provide more control and more ability to customize than a hosted blogging service.

Dollar Stretcher

Most domain name registrars offer a discount on registration fees if you purchase more than one year at a time. If you're sure you want to keep the selected domain for a while, buy a few years up front to save money.

If you need to register a domain name, you'll choose this method of running a blog, and you'll likely have to pay hosting fees. This method may be more expensive for you in the beginning, but as your blog grows, your expenses won't grow with it the way they would with a blogging service. That means that as your advertising or merchandising revenue rises, your profits won't be eaten up by higher service fees.

If you have no familiarity with hosting a website and the process seems daunting, do some research before choosing this path. It can be trying at times for those unfamiliar with web hosting, but it can certainly be learned and is worth the time it takes to get up to speed—especially if you plan on making your living running a website.

When seeking a blogging platform, be sure to consider your intended content. In most cases, a blog is simply text, links and the occasional photo. So, in most cases, any blog service you choose will be able to handle all the content you need. But as the blogging phenomenon has expanded, so have bloggers' requirements. To keep up with the competition, you may need your blog to play sound clips, videos and more. Be sure to check out the feature lists of any blog platform you wish to use.

Typical Staffing Needs

The blogging business has lots of parts. There's the actual blogging, of course, but there's also advertising, marketing, accounting, merchandising and so on. Blogging is a fun business, but it's still a real business and needs to be treated as such. No one person can run a reliable, successful, profitable business that serves the needs of thousands (or millions) of customers every day—which yours will hopefully do. As the business is getting started, your main goal should be to run a reliable blog while planning the business's growth. You shouldn't assume that you can do everything the business needs for as long as the business needs it.

In the beginning, you'll probably do everything yourself. But there will come a point when you simply can't do everything you need to do in the course of the day. In addition to researching and writing posts for your blog, you may also be responsible for soliciting advertisers, managing advertising networks, processing merchandise orders, e-mailing readers, and a thousand other little things. And that long list doesn't even include all the responsibilities of your nonblogging personal life. As your business grows, taking care of all the peripheral work that building a successful blog requires, while posting frequently and reliably on the blog, will become impossible. Before you become overwhelmed by the amount of work required to keep your blog going—and definitely if you notice the quality of your posts suffering because you're too busy with the "back office" part of your business—it's time to hire help.

The first type of employees you might think of hiring are contributors to generate additional content for your blog. Contributors typically are paid a small stipend—anywhere from $5 to $25, but sometimes more—per post.

If you only need occasional help generating content, you may also find it possible to "swap" duties with other bloggers. That is, you generate posts for their site when they're unavailable, and they do the same for you. Some bloggers are willing to do this to generate publicity and attract new readers to their own blogs.

The additional types of employees you may need will depend on the tasks you envision taking up most of your time as your blog grows. If you're selling merchandise, consider part-time shipping help. If you're selling advertising space to private sponsors, consider a part-time marketer to attract more advertisers. Once you get help with the most time-consuming areas of your business, you'll have some free time to devote to the other areas that require your attention.

Money Matters

We have good news and bad news about the financial aspects of running a blog. The good news is that you can start a blog for next to nothing. Unfortunately, "next to nothing" might also be a way to describe your profits. But it is possible to make money as a blogger.

Startup Costs and Income Potential

You can start your own blog with—quite literally—no money at all. This assumes, of course, that you already have a computer and internet access. If you don't have either, you can purchase a very basic computer for less than $500 and get high-speed internet access for about $45 per month. If you pay for a blogging service, you can expect to shell out $5 to $10 for your first month; to cut costs initially, you can launch using a free service.

You can see a complete breakdown of the estimated startup costs for launching both a big-time blogging business and a basic blog in the chart on page 70. A Basic Blog is a single blog run by an individual, while a Big-Time Blog Biz can be a network of blogs run either alone or with a partner. You also can use the work sheet on page 71 to calculate your own startup expenses.

With such a modest investment, how much money can you make? "Income potential varies so greatly," Rob May notes. "Of 55 million blogs, maybe 5,000 of them generate enough money to live off of."

May estimates that with some time and effort, you can begin to make about $1,000 per month from your blog. But getting to that point takes a while; in his first month displaying advertising, May says he made $23.

There's good news, however. "Getting to that point [making $1,000 a month] is very hard. But from there, it goes up very quickly," May says. In some ways, it's much more difficult to get to the point of making $1,000 a month than it is to get to the point where you're making $10,000 per month, he notes.

But with some hard work, persistence and plenty of patience, you can make it there, too.

Sample Startup Costs

Item	Basic Blog	Big-Time Blog Biz
Office rent and utilities	$0	$0
Desktop/laptop computers	$500	$1,000
Software	$0	$9
Office supplies/equipment	$100	$700
Internet access	$45	$45
Phone service	$0	$45
Doman name registration	$9	$9
Web hosting	$0	$7
Contributors	$0	$0*
Subtotal	$654	$1,815
Miscellaneous expenses (10 percent of subtotal)	$65	$181
Total Costs	**$719**	**$1,996**

*At startup, you won't need contributors.

Startup Expenses Worksheet

Item	Estimate
Office rent and utilities	$
Desktop/laptop computers	$
Software	$
Office supplies/equipment	$
Internet access	$
Phone service	$
Doman name registration	$
Web hosting	$
Contributors	$
Subtotal	$
Miscellaneous expenses (10 percent of subtotal)	$
Total Costs	$

6

Make a
Plan

You're getting ready to start an internet service, so your business will be virtual. You're not selling a packaged product; you're selling an idea or a concept, or even advice. But even though your business may be centered in cyberspace, you still need to use some good, old-fashioned business principles to get ready for your launch. We're talking about market research and business plans.

Do Your Market Research

Many entrepreneurs will head out to their local neighborhoods to see if their town can support another small business. If they're planning on launching an ice cream parlor, they can tour the neighborhood, look for competition, and see if a new place might be welcomed. Launching a net service is slightly different; you can't take a walk around the block exactly, but you still want to make sure you know who you'll be competing with and if the business landscape has room for one more competitor.

Identifying Your Competition

Let's start with how to identify that competition. Your business is online so that's where you're going to be conducting much of your market research.

"The first thing you want to do is a Google search," says Rick Marini, who co-founded Tickle.com. "If you're thinking of launching a company that offers digital music downloads, type in 'digital music downloads' and see what comes up."

From there, you can research each of the companies you find. Using a research tool like Alexa.com, you can find out who owns the domain and how much traffic the site gets. You can also see the site's traffic in a historical context—whether it has gone up

Dollar Stretcher

Don't pay someone else to do market research that you can perform. Use all the free online resources you can find—including Google, Alexa and Whois—to scope out your competition.

or down over the past several months. You also can find out how these companies are funded and how big they are. This can help you determine if there's room for another site, like the one you're planning to launch.

"If you're really new and you don't know the landscape at all, you may want to do a survey. But I don't necessarily think it's the best use of time and money to hire a company and do a survey," Marini says. "My market research is more anecdotal."

Your time could be better spent simply talking to people in the industry, he says. One way to start is to find someone who works in the industry—or even a related industry—and listen to what they have to say. They can provide insight on what works and what doesn't.

One important step in your market research is to find out how the companies you'll be competing with make their money. If your field is SEM or website design, the answer is obvious: They make money by charging their clients. But if you're launching a new media service that will be free to end users, the answer may not be as clear. So ask around, look into as many public records as you can, and find out how the companies generate funds.

> **⚠ Beware!**
> Many entrepreneurs turn to their friends and family when looking for opinions on business ideas, but you're better off asking someone else. Your mother means well, but her response may be overly enthusiastic and skewed in your favor.

Just because a market may be crowded doesn't mean there isn't any room for you, Marini notes. But there are a couple of things to consider before jumping in head first. "Is it still an industry that's making money? How is the money distributed? Is there one company that's making all the money?" says Marini. If one company is making all the money, it may be a sign that you should avoid this area. For example, we mentioned digital music downloads. Apple makes much of the money in this industry with its iTunes music store. Do you really want to compete with that—and is it even possible?

But if you see a market where there are only a few competitors and you see that revenue is available, it makes sense to enter. There's a bonus to joining a market that's already been carved out by someone else, Marini notes: "They've already done the research, so you can be a fast follower. You can grow what they've already put into motion."

You may also be the first one in the market—but there may be a reason why no one else is there. Marini notes, "Being the first means you are either really smart or really dumb."

Identify Your Niche

As someone offering a net service, you should be considered an expert in that field. Whether you're blogging about a topic or optimizing a website for search engines, you can sell yourself based on your knowledge and credibility.

For example, when selecting a topic for your blog, you should choose a topic that isn't so large that your expertise isn't plausible. Few people will ever be considered experts on the gigantic topic of "sports," but it's certainly possible for you to be considered an expert on a narrower niche like the NBA. Likewise, it's doubtful that any one person will be considered an expert on "animals." It's more believable that someone is an expert on "dog training."

You can apply these same principles to launching the other types of net services described in this book. If you're interested in web design, consider what you can offer that your competitors can't. Perhaps you can prepare print collateral for companies—such as letterhead and brochures—

> **Tip...**
> **Smart Tip**
> One way to establish credibility—and to make room for yourself in a crowded market—is to find a niche.

in addition to designing websites. If you're getting ready to launch a new social networking service, look at the ones currently in existence and see what they're missing. Facebook is skewed toward the younger crowd (though, really, its target audience seems to be the internet population at large), while LinkedIn takes on the business crowd. Perhaps you could target new parents or sports car enthusiasts with your service?

For more help with market research, see "Choose Your Target" and "If You Build It, Will They Come?" chapters in *Startup Basics*.

> ⚠ **Beware!**
> You don't want to limit yourself by thinking too small, so you should carefully consider your niche market when designing your service. If you can strike a balance and find a niche that allows you to develop and deliver your expertise, you'll have a better chance of wooing your clients.

Who Is Your Clientele?

Now it's time to talk about those clients. This book looks at four net services: web design, SEM, new media and blogs. Certainly, the clientele for these services will vary greatly. But for the purposes of our discussion, we're going to split these into two groups: blogs/new media online services and web design/SEM. Blogs and new media services are likely to be free services that generate revenue primarily through advertising. Web design and SEM firms will charge their customers for the services they provide.

Clientele for Blogs/New Media Online Services

You may have come to this book with an idea for your new service in place. That is, you may already know the topic of your blog or what type of new media service you're going to offer. If that's the case, you may also know who your clientele will be. If you're offering a new media service or blog centered on skateboarding, for instance, you may already know that your clientele—or your target audience—is teenage boys. If you're blogging about restaurants in a certain area, your target audience will likely be locals or people who plan to visit the area.

But if you don't know your topic yet or the focus of your new media service, you should spend some time thinking about your advertisers. This is how you will eventually make your money, so you want to make sure you have a desirable audience that you can deliver to your advertisers.

"Before you launch your company, you should identify your potential customers, users and advertisers," Marini says. "First, match your content with who you think your advertisers will be. You can think specifically, if I have a content site for teen

Will Blog for Money

Not yet set on a topic for your blog? Here are a few tips on selecting a topic that can produce desirable profits for you.

You need to select a topic that has good advertising potential; blogs about commodity items, such as digital cameras and MP3 players, for example, provide more advertising options and often more advertising revenue. You also should consider public interest, your knowledge of the topic and the longevity of the subject.

Remember: Your goal is to attract millions of visitors every month, and therefore blogging about provincial or tiny niche topics may not serve you well. For example, a blog that addresses the political happenings in your town of 30,000 people may very well become the hottest thing in town, but the audience topic has a ceiling. Realistically, it's likely that only 1 out of every 10 people in your town have the time or interest to read blogs in the course of a day, and of those few people, even fewer are interested in town politics. So while it may excite you personally, the reality is that this topic is limited.

boys, who will my advertisers be? Skateboard companies, video games, etc. Then you can go from there."

Rob May, the blogger behind BusinessPundit.com, says one strategy for planning a blog is to look at topic niches. "You could focus all your time on finding unexploited niches. If you figure out which niches you can target, you could try to sell ads for a higher price."

Whatever you do, Marini has two words of advice: Think big. "Think about the general categories of advertisers that will fit with the content. You have to have broad categories," he says. "For every 10 potential advertisers that walk through the door, you'll be lucky to close two or three."

Bright Idea

Use your company's small size to your advantage. Remind your clients that they'll get more personalized service from you than a bigger company can offer.

Clientele for Web Design/SEM

When you're designing websites or running search marketing campaigns, you're going to charge your clients for the services you're offering. So you're not looking at your audience in terms of what an advertiser sees, as you would if you were launching a blog or a new media service. Instead, what you need to consider is the size and scope of the projects you can successfully handle for your clients. You also need to consider your physical location and that of your potential clients; you may not always need to meet your clients face to face, but you may want to have it as an option.

As a new business, you'll probably have to start small when it comes to clients. Bigger businesses may not be as willing to take a chance on a new company, and you may not be able to offer them all the services they need. If you're a solo website designer who can't add e-commerce functionality to a site, you're not going to be an attractive option to a mid-sized company looking to sell products online. That doesn't mean there isn't a market for your business; you simply need to understand your limitations and target your services to clients who are a good fit.

As you grow, you can expand your skill set—and with it, your clientele. Do remember that if you promise something to a client, you must make sure you can deliver it. Notes UpWord SEM's Robert Cavilla, "You live and die off your client referrals."

You should also keep in mind that as a small business, you can win big clients. In fact, smaller shops may have an advantage over their bigger competitors: "Your clients may appreciate knowing they're working with a senior partner at your company. They may feel they get more attention that way," Cavilla says.

You don't always need to meet your clients in person, but doing so is one way to differentiate yourself in a crowded market. "Most of our communication with clients is done through e-mail and conference calls. We have clients all over the country," Cavilla says of his Boston-based business. "But we value our relationships and we try to meet with all of them in person at least once. Some clients we meet with regularly."

There can be downsides to meeting your clients in person, however. "It may be easier to sell people on your ideas if you're meeting in person, but it's easy to end up wasting time," notes Todd Mailcoat, the SEO consultant who writes a blog on SEM at Stuntdubl.com. "It's easy to get caught up in providing favors and wasting time on needless meetings. Over the phone, it's easier to get right down to business."

How you choose to meet with your clients will likely depend on their own comfort level and the status of your business. You may find it necessary to meet face to face while you're still establishing your company and building your reputation. Once your services can sell themselves, you may no longer need to do so—unless both you and your clients prefer it that way.

How to Write Your Business Plan

Some people would have you believe that the internet is going to kill off paper. While the environment appreciates this idea, your business can still benefit from the use of good, old-fashioned paper—that's where you should put your business plan.

A business plan conveys your business goals and the strategies you'll use to meet them; potential problems that may confront your business and the ways you'll solve them; the organizational structure of your business (including job titles and responsibilities); and the amount of capital required to finance your venture and keep it going until it breaks even.

What Your Plan Needs

If put together correctly, a business plan can be very impressive. When compiling your plan, there are three primary parts you should consider.

The first is the *business concept*, where you discuss the industry, your business structure, your product or service, and how you plan to make your business a success. The second is the *marketplace* section, where you describe and analyze your potential customers. Here you would also describe the competition and how you will position yourself to beat it. The last section is the *financial* section, which contains your income and cash-flow statement, balance sheet and other financial ratios, such as break-even analyses.

These three major sections provide only a general outline. More specifically, a business plan consists of seven key components:

1. Executive summary
2. Business description
3. Market strategies
4. Competitive analysis
5. Design and development plan
6. Operations and management plan
7. Financial factors

In addition to these sections, a business plan should have a cover, title page and a table of contents.

> ### Smart Tip
> **Tip...**
>
> Your business plan shouldn't only identify your potential users and advertisers; it also should earmark your potential purchasers. Your plan may be to take your company public, but the chances of that happening are remote. You should know who could—and should—acquire you.

Executive Summary

Anyone looking at your business plan will first want to know what kind of business you're starting. So the business concept section should start with an executive summary, which outlines and describes your net service.

The executive summary is the first thing the reader sees, so it should make an immediate impact. It should clearly state the nature of the business and, if you're seeking capital, the type of financing you want. (We'll discuss types of funding in Chapter 8.)

The executive summary describes your net service, its legal form of operation (sole proprietorship, partnership, corporation or limited liability corporation), the amount and purpose of the loan requested, the repayment schedule, the borrower's equity share, and the debt-to-equity ratio after the loan, security or collateral is offered. Also listed are the market and estimated values, or any price quotes for any equipment you plan to purchase with the loan proceeds.

Your executive summary should be short and businesslike—generally between half a page and one page, depending on how complicated the use of funds is.

Business Description

This section expands on your executive summary, describing your net service in much greater detail. It usually starts with a description of your industry. Describe the size of the industry, explain why it has grown so popular, and discuss the trends that have been responsible for that growth. Use statistics and anecdotal information to prove how much opportunity is available in your industry, whether you're starting a web design company, an SEM firm, a new media service or a blog.

You should identify the target market for your service, how you'll deliver that service to your clients, and the business' support systems—that is, the advertising, promotions and customer service strategies.

Next, you should describe your specific service in detail, including how it will be used by your clients and who the end users are. For example, if you're launching an SEM agency, you should explain the type of advice you will deliver to your clients and the steps you'll take to help them implement your suggested changes. If you're planning to launch an online photo-sharing service, you should discuss its key features. Explain what your target audience will be able to do with it. Emphasize any unique features or variations that set your service apart from others in the industry.

If you're using your business plan to seek funding, explain how that money will make your business more profitable. Be specific. Will you use the money to expand your service, to buy new equipment, or to hire more employees?

The key in this section—and throughout your business plan—is to remain very focused. "Your business idea should be directed toward a very focused market. A general idea doesn't necessarily plan out all that well, particularly if you're late coming to market," says Jessica Canning, director of global research with Dow

Smart Tip

Be as specific as possible when writing your business plan. If you're seeking funding, explain in detail how you'll use the money. If you're describing your competition, explain what they offer—and what you'll offer that they don't. Use statistics to prove your point wherever possible.

Jones VentureSource. "Not all internet companies are late, but the competitive landscape is increasing every day. It's increasingly difficult to differentiate yourself. Investors look at how your company is different."

Market Strategies

This is the first component of the marketplace section, which will focus on your customers and your competition. Here's where you define your market—its size, structure, growth prospects, trends and sales potential. How much of that market will your service be able to capture?

The answer will be tricky to determine because so many variables influence it. Think of it as a combination of words and numbers. Write down the who, what, when, where and why of your customers. These answers are critical in determining how you'll develop pricing strategies (if you're charging your clients) and distribution channels.

Be sure to document how and from what sources you compiled your market information. Describe how your net service fits into the overall market picture. Emphasize your unique selling proposition (USP)—in other words, what makes you different? Explain why your approach is ideal for your market.

Once you've clearly defined your market and established your sales goals, present the strategies you'll use to meet those goals.

- **Price:** For web design and SEM businesses that will charge their clients, as well as any new media or blogging services that will charge users for subscriptions, thoroughly explain your pricing strategy and how it will affect the success of your service. Describe your projected costs (including overhead, advertising and equipment) and then determine pricing based on the profit percentage you expect. Many experts advise adding 25 to 50 percent to each cost estimate, especially overhead, to ensure you don't underestimate.
- **Distribution:** If you were selling a physical product, this is where you'd describe the entire process of moving your product from the factory to the end user. Because you're offering a service, you should describe how your service will be delivered to your target audience or clientele. If you're offering a new media service, for example, how will you get that service up and running on a website? If you're selling web design services, how will your clients get the end results?
- **Sales:** Explain how your sales force (if you have one) will meet its goals, including elements such as pricing flexibility, sales presentations and lead generation. You should also include information on compensation policies.

Competitive Analysis

How does your business relate to the competition? The competitive analysis section answers this question. Using what you've learned from your market research, detail the strengths and weaknesses of your competitors, the strategies that give you a distinct advantage, any barriers you can develop to prevent new competition from entering the market, and any weaknesses in your competitors' service that you can take advantage of.

The competitive analysis is an important part of your business plan. Often, startup entrepreneurs mistakenly believe that their service is the first of its kind and fail to recognize that competition exists. In reality, every business has competition, whether it's direct or indirect.

Beware!
Don't assume—or try to convince anyone—that your net service has no competition. You may think this sounds like a good selling point, but it makes you look naïve.

"One of the most common mistakes people make is saying they have no competitors. If you're launching an online business and you don't have Google, Microsoft and Yahoo! on your map as your competitors, you're overlooking something," says VentureSource's Canning.

"Take a critical look at your business plan, especially your potential competitors. Describe, as specifically as you can, how you will adapt if your competitor changes. How are you going to adapt if you're a social networking site and a competitor like Facebook launches? Describe how you'll adapt if you don't meet your revenue streams. You want to be able to prove that you've thought this out," Canning says. "A track record is really important. If you can give examples of how you've adapted in the past, it will help you gain funding."

Development Plan

For an internet service, your development plan will cover market and organizational development. You should create a schedule that shows how your service, marketing strategies and organization will develop over time. The schedule should be tied to a development budget so expenses can be tracked throughout the process.

Operations and Management Plan

Here, you'll describe how your business will function on a daily basis. This section explains logistics such as the responsibilities of each member of the management team, the tasks assigned to each division of the company (if applicable), and the capital and expense requirements for operating the business.

Describe the business's managers and their qualifications, and specify what type of support staff will be necessary for the business to run efficiently. Any potential benefits or pitfalls of a net service should also be discussed, including the possible need to hire remote workers and how you'll retain employees in a competitive internet environment.

Financial Factors

The financial statements are the backbone of your business plan. They show how profitable your net service will be in the short and long term, and should include the following:

The *income statement* details the business's cash-generating ability. It projects such items as revenue, expenses, capital (in the form of depreciation), and cost of goods.

Ad Sense

Some of the net services we talk about in this book will rely on advertising as their primary source of revenue. That very thought may have you recalling the ghosts of dotcom startups gone bust. But it shouldn't: Handled the right way, advertising can indeed be a source of revenue.

"Online advertising is a viable business model; there's a lot more money in it now," says Jon Gibs, vice president of media analytics with Nielsen Online. Just how much more money is in internet advertising? According to a recent study by the Yankee Group, the online advertising market in the United States will reach $50.3 billion by 2011. Clearly, money is being spent on online advertising.

Don't let those numbers make you giddy, however. As Gibs says, "You can succeed with advertising, but the odds are against you."

If you're planning on launching a net service that generates its revenue primarily from advertising, you'd do well to follow the model used by offline publishers. "A web startup based on an advertising platform is much closer to a publishing company," Gibs says. You have to remember that not only are you delivering content, but you're also delivering advertising. Having a unique content model isn't enough, he says. You have to constantly think of how you can attract a unique audience that you can deliver to advertisers.

"Ad dollars come to people who can deliver a unique audience. Reach is important, too, but as a small company, you should focus on being able to deliver an audience to your advertisers that can't be delivered otherwise," says Gibs.

One piece of advice that Gibs offers: Go for the thinnest niche audience you can while still maintaining an audience. He notes, "You may only have a small audience, but you can make your audience very valuable."

You should generate a monthly income statement for the business's first year, quarterly statements for the second year, and annual statements for each year thereafter, usually for the next five years.

The *cashflow* statement details the amount of money coming into and going out of the business—monthly for the first year and quarterly for each year thereafter. The result is a profit or loss at the end of the period represented by each column. Both profits and losses carry over to the last column to show a cumulative amount. If your cash-flow statement shows you consistently operating at a loss, you'll probably need additional cash to meet expenses. Most businesses—even net services—have some seasonal variations in their budgets, so re-examine your cash-flow calculations if they look identical every month.

The *balance sheet* paints a picture of the business's financial strength in terms of assets, liabilities and equity over a set period. You should generate a balance sheet for every year profiled in the development of your business.

After these essential financial documents, include any relevant summary information that's not included elsewhere in the plan but will significantly affect business. This could include ratios such as return on investment (ROI), break-even point or return on assets. Your accountant can help you decide which information is best to include.

A business plan is a necessity if you're seeking funding for your business, but it's not just a tool used to obtain financing—it's a guide to help you define and meet your business goals. Researching and refining your business plan will point out weak spots in your business idea that you'll be able to repair.

Planning Ahead

Your business plan also allows you to plan ahead to a time when your business will grow. If you're starting a relatively modest blog at home in your spare time, such a detailed business plan may seem silly and unnecessary. But you always want to plan ahead and think as big as you can.

Countdown to Startup

Thinking big is something you should be doing when you're planning to launch your company. This means that you shouldn't consider only the equipment and employees that you need today but what you'll need six months from now.

Let's use a blogging business as an example. Today, a hosted blogging service may offer everything you need. It may offer built-in, but limited, advertising capabilities. This, obviously, has real benefits when you're just starting out. But once your blog begins drawing serious traffic and you outgrow that simple advertising strategy, it

A Little Help from Your Friends

A business plan isn't worth very much to your business if you never take the time to revisit it. You should be constantly updating your plan and adjusting the operations of your business to make sure you're meeting the goals you've set. You don't have to drag out a paper copy of your plan to do this, however: A web service called PlanHQ (planhq.com) can help.

PlanHQ lets you create a web-based, collaborative business plan that can be accessed by people both inside and outside your company. You can use the site to set goals and deadlines for them, track your markets and your competitors, view a graphical summary of your financial performance, and track the activities of your workgroup.

The site isn't a replacement for the traditional business plan you'll need to present to potential investors and bankers when you apply for a loan. But it can help transform your business plan into a living document that does more than just sit in a desk drawer.

could cause problems for you. Integration of outside ad networks may not be allowed or, if allowed, could be a technical pain to implement.

Advertising isn't the only area where you should be concerned about growth. You should also consider growth in terms of blog traffic and storage space. If you choose to use a hosted blogging service, it may have traffic and storage maximums—especially for its free service. You may find out that as you grow, so will the fees you owe, which may or may not be a deciding factor for you.

How can you apply this same principle to the other types of net services? Keep your potential growth in mind when selecting everything from the software you need (will you get a discount on purchasing multiple licenses?) to the office space you lease (is there room to expand if you need to add more employees?).

Setting a Timeframe for Your Goals

Getting ready to launch your company and preparing to deliver your net service are two distinct things. As we discussed in each of the chapters on the specific businesses you can start, you'll need to allow for some time to gain traction in the marketplace. Just how long should you wait? It will likely depend on the type of net service you're starting, but in most cases, industry experts say you should give yourself about a year.

If you're launching a blog or a new media service, you should expect it to take about three months for search engines—and therefore web searchers—to realize you exist (and this may be after months spent in development and in your beta period).

Once search engines have found you, it will still take some time to grow, but you should see a steadily increasing stream of traffic. If you don't see traffic increasing, you should take a hard look at what you're offering and wonder why.

The same can be said for launching a web design firm or a SEM service. Realize that it may take several months to build your portfolio and reputation. But keep slogging away.

Beware!
You want to allow a reasonable amount of time for your business to grow, but you can't be too lax. If you find that you're not meeting the goals you've set, try to figure out why. Even in the early days, you must be vigilant.

A year is a good estimate for a net service with modest goals; if your ambitions are grander, you may want to allow for more time. But if at any point you find that your traffic or business is slipping away, you should immediately try to find out why and see what you can do about it.

Startup Checklist

Task	Completed
Conduct market research (identify your customers and competitors)	
Create a business plan	
Create a marketing plan	
Choose a name for your business	
Register your domain name	
Select a legal structure	
Find a lawyer	
Create your business (by incorporating or forming your partnership or LLC)	
Register your business name with your state and/or city	
Find an accountant	
Get a federal employer ID number	
Get a state tax identification number	
Find a banker	
Open a business checking account	
Obtain funding; apply for loans and find investors	
Find an insurance agent	
Get insurance coverage	
Research any government or insurance regulations you may face, such as unemployment insurance or self-employment tax	
Apply for any necessary trademarks/patents/copyright protections	
Lease office space	
Purchase necessary equipment and supplies	
Price your services	
Have contracts and forms reviewed by your attorney	
Set up a line of credit	

Startup Checklist (continued)

Task	Completed
Set up a bookkeeping and invoicing system	
Design or hire someone to design business cards and company marketing materials	
Advertise	
Open for business!	

Making It
Official

Your plan is in place. You've identified your competition, prospective clients and target market. You're ready to go. It's time to become an official business.

Structuring Your Business

As an honest-to-goodness, real-life business, you will (at some point!) be making money. Therefore, you'll be paying taxes. And few decisions will affect the way you pay your taxes more than how you structure your business. There are several types of business classifications to choose from, each with benefits and drawbacks.

Choosing a Legal Structure

The "Making It Legal" chapter in *Startup Basics* offers a detailed explanation of the various structures you might choose for your business. Here's a brief overview, with some added notes on how these structures may relate to your net service.

- **Sole proprietorship:** A sole proprietorship is the most common type of startup business because it requires little paperwork. You're the only owner. Legally, financially and tax-wise, there's no difference between you and your business. Your business assets are your assets. Your business debt is your personal debt. And your business profits are your income.

  This structure will likely appeal to bloggers and web designers who plan to work alone. It's also an option for SEM professionals who intend to work in a consulting capacity on their own. It may not work, however, for new media services, which are likely to have more employees. Remember that if you plan on adding employees later on, you may want to select another structure. But if you know that you'll be a lone wolf, a sole proprietorship can make sense.

  > **Tip...**
  >
  > **Smart Tip**
  > Starting as a sole proprietor can be a good move. It's inexpensive and easy. Just be aware that you'll be without the legal protections other business structures enjoy.

  The advantages to this type of business are that it's easy to start and you keep all the profits for yourself. You need only to file a business income form (Schedule C) along with your regular taxes. The disadvantage of this type of business is that you're personally liable for all the business's debt and mistakes. If your company is sued for any reason, you're directly sued.

- **Partnership:** A partnership is similar to a sole proprietorship, except instead of one proprietor, there are two. Both parties are legally and financially responsible for the business. Some partnerships are based on common interests (such as husband-wife teams), and some are based on financial need (such as the financier and the manager).

If you're interested in setting up a partnership, be excruciatingly clear going into the business about who will take on what role, who makes what decisions, and who receives what money. A clearly defined relationship will go a long way toward making the business relationship a success.

- **Corporation:** Unlike a sole proprietorship or partnership, a corporation is its own legal entity. A corporation's debt, taxes, profits and legal liability are separate from the corporation owner. While this provides immense protection for owners, corporations can be expensive to get started. If you're interested in starting a corporation, you should contact an attorney in your area for help.

Bloggers who are running just one blog and web design professionals who are working alone may not need to set up a corporation. But if you're considering expanding into two, four or 14 blogs, or are planning to grow your web design firm down the road, adding employees and considerable revenue, you may require the protection that a corporation provides.

> **Smart Tip**
> Finding a partner with complementary skills can be an excellent way to grow your business, especially if you find someone who adds skills that you lack.

- **S corporation:** An S corporation is an alternative for small businesses that are interested in incorporation. It provides significant financial and legal benefits for small-business owners. Like a regular corporation, an S corporation is its own entity, and its legal liabilities and debts are separate from those of its owners.

Unlike a corporation, which taxes owners twice—once as corporate income tax and once on owner dividends—an S corporation doesn't pay taxes on its corporate income. It's treated almost like a sole proprietorship or partnership for tax purposes. The profits of the S corporation are passed on to its shareholders, who then pay income tax on those profits.

There are some limitations to S corporations, however: Your company can have only one class of stock and you are limited to 75 shareholders. Those shareholders must be individuals (or an estate or a trust) who are U.S. residents; other corporations cannot be stockholders.

- **Limited liability company:** Like an S corporation, limited liability companies (LLCs) provide owners with legal and financial protection, while avoiding the double taxation that occurs in corporations. This is quickly becoming the default choice for small businesses—and a smart decision for self-publishers such as bloggers. If you publish any sort of material that could be considered libelous, you should protect your personal assets by setting up an LLC.

Setting up an LLC is relatively easy as well. Talk to your state's Secretary of State's office about where to obtain the necessary forms.

▲

Getting Your Federal ID

Depending on the structure and the operations of your net service, you may need to apply for an employer identification number (EIN) with the federal government. This is almost like a Social Security number for your business; it identifies your business as a tax-paying entity to the government. (It is sometimes called a tax identification number, or a TIN.)

If you operate your business as a corporation or a partnership, you'll need an EIN. Some sole proprietors and LLCs will require EINs as well—if you have employees, you'll need an EIN, for example. The IRS offers a basic questionnaire on its website (irs.gov) that will help you determine if you need an EIN. If you do, you can apply for one through that website as well.

Picking a Name

New parents debate baby names for months—even years—before planting the perfect moniker on their newborn. You may not have that much time to decide on the perfect name for your new business, but you do want to put the same weight on the decision. The name of your company is the first thing many advertisers and potential customers will hear, so you want to make a good first impression.

"A name needs to be descriptive, spellable, memorable. It's nice if it's evocative, if it causes some sort of emotion when you hear it, like Yahoo!," says Tickle's Rick Marini. "Amazon was used to convey something that was huge. Google is unique and memorable now, and it's spellable."

While the name of a blog or new media online service may need to evoke emotion from potential site visitors and advertisers, the name of an SEM company or web design firm should project professionalism to potential clients. You want your clients to know that you're not a fly-by-night operation, and one way to establish a good impression is with your name. Many companies use the name of their founders to project a professional image from the start.

> **⚠ Beware!**
> Don't select a name that may be offensive to anyone, no matter how witty you think it is. You may alienate more potential clients than you amuse.

Before you can decide on any sort of name, however, you need to make sure the URL is available. As a net service, your company will be living on the internet. Just as an offline company—like a restaurant—needs to find a location that's easily accessible to its customers, you need to find the perfect online home. Finding an available URL is key.

You can find out if a URL is available by typing the name directly into your web browser, or trying to register it through a domain registrar like GoDaddy.com. If a

Bright Idea

Don't just think about your business name—think about a tagline, too. Todd Mailcoat's SEM consulting firm, called Stuntdubl, uses the tagline "Getting hit by traffic, not cars." The tagline cleverly explains the meaning of his company's name and ties it into his industry, while also providing a few laughs.

domain is taken, you can use a service such as Whois (whois.net) to find out who owns the rights to that name. If you're very interested in a name that's taken, you can attempt to purchase the rights to the domain from the existing owner. But if that's beyond your budget, you can look for an alternative.

Most experts agree that one alternative you should try to avoid is veering away from a .com extension on your domain name. With so many URLs already taken, it may be tempting to look for an available URL with another extension like .net or .biz, but you should avoid this if at all possible. A .com extension is more reputable, looks better to clients and advertisers, and will rank better in search engines. Ideally, you want to acquire all the extensions that go along with the URL you choose, but you definitely want the .com extension first and foremost.

One way internet companies are getting around the lack of available URLs is by creating new words to use as company names. While that worked well for Google, it's not always the best bet. Marini's first company was originally named eMode.com, but four-and-a-half years into the venture, the name was changed to Tickle.

"We used eMode because we were trying to say emotion and the mode of your

Ask and You Shall Receive

Need help coming up with a name for your net service? Just ask for it.

WordLab's Wordboard Naming Forums (wordlab.com/wordboard) let you post requests for other users to suggest names for your company or to evaluate names you're considering. The site also lets you ask for help naming specific services and coming up with taglines. The site is free, though some users do offer rewards should someone come up with a name they end up using.

You can also hire a professional firm to help you name your company, but that can be too expensive for many startups. Fees can range from a few thousand dollars to upwards of $30,000. If you have the funds, though, a consultant can help you create the perfect name for your company and has the know-how to navigate the confusing laws surrounding trademarks and copyrights.

life," Marini says of the personality-testing site. "But at a cocktail party, we'd say the name and people thought we were saying eloan or emote. So we changed it to Tickle."

Robert Cavilla says his company, UpWord SEM, also went through a name change. The company was initially called Blue Reef Consulting, but shortly after they launched, they were contacted by a company in Florida that was operating under the same name. The company sent them a cease-and-desist letter, claiming trademark violations.

Cavilla says that he and his partner decided on a new name through a brainstorming session. "We wrote down a lot of words related to what we did. We move words up and down, so we came up with UpWord," he says. He says people do sometimes misspell the name but says he's happy with it overall and has it trademarked.

While these examples show that it's possible to change your company name once you start, it's not always easy. Changing your name can alienate customers and destroy any brand equity that you've built. So try to get it right from the start.

Registering Your Business Name

It may be necessary for you to register your business name with your state before you can do such things as open a business bank account or apply for a bank loan. Registering your business name also ensures that you have the rights to that name in your state. Other companies will still be able to operate under the same name, but if it ever came to a legal battle, you would have a claim. Registration is a simple process that involves a form, a small processing fee and a stamp. Check with your state's Secretary of State's website for more information.

If your business is structured as a corporation, LLC or partnership, your business name may have been automatically registered during that process. If you plan to operate your business under a name that's different from its legal name, you need to register a dba, which stands for "doing business as," with your state or county as well. This is sometimes called a "fictitious name"—that is, it doesn't include either the legal name of the person or entity that owns the business.

Protecting Your Assets

Now that you've selected a structure and named your business, it's time to protect what you have.

Copyrights, Trademarks and Patents

As the owner of a net service, what you have that's worth protecting is your intellectual property, which can be defined as "a collection of ideas and concepts." How do you protect that? The government offers various methods for protecting your intellectual property: patents, copyrights and trademarks. As the owner of a net service, you're also likely to be interested in service marks, which are similar to trademarks. Here are the definitions of these protections, according to the U.S. Patent and Trademark Office (PTO):

Smart Tip

If the name you're interested in is already trademarked by a company in another industry, you may still be able to use it. The U.S. Patent & Trademark Office may allow companies in different industries to use the same name, so it's worth looking into.

- **Patent:** A property right granted by the U.S. government to an inventor "to exclude others from making, using, offering for sale, or selling the invention."

- **Copyright:** Protects works of authorship, such as writings, music and works of art, that have been tangibly expressed.

- **Trademark:** Protects words, names, symbols, sounds or colors that distinguish goods and services from those manufactured or sold by others; is used to indicate the source of the goods.

- **Service mark:** A word, name, symbol or device that indicates the source of the services and distinguishes them from the services of others. A service mark is the same as a trademark, except it identifies and distinguishes the source of a service rather than a product.

How do these apply to your net service? First off, you need to make sure that no one else has trademarked the name or logo you're interested in using for your business. You can search existing trademarks at the U.S. PTO website (uspto.gov). If the name you want is already trademarked, you'll need to find another one. As soon as you find one that's trademark-free, you should file an application to trademark it yourself. You can do this at uspto.gov, too; the site provides detailed instructions to guide you through the entire process.

In general, you should try to trademark any company names or logos that will be used to identify your company. You'll also want to service mark any names, phrases or logos used to identify the specific services you're offering.

Beware!

Don't assume that your net service doesn't need copyright protection. Any original content you create and post online may benefit from it.

Patents are used to protect "new and useful" inventions. Most people assume that patents are only granted to protect physical inventions, not virtual processes like those of your net service. But patents have been applied to web services in the past: Amazon, for example, has patented several features available on its shopping site, including its 1-Click purchasing tool

▲

and a customer recommendation feature. So depending on what type of service you're offering, you may be able to protect it with patents. If you think you need a patent, you definitely need an experienced attorney who can guide you through the process.

If your net service will involve posting content on your site, you need the protection of a copyright. This doesn't just go for those of you planning to run a blogging business; it also pertains to anyone starting a new media service that may involve posting original work online, an SEM firm that will be creating original content for their clients' websites, a website designer creating his own graphics, or a website designer or search engine marketer writing articles or books to build reputation within their industry. Your work is copyrighted as soon as "it is created and fixed in a tangible form that is perceptible either directly or with the aid of a machine or device," according to Copyright.gov.

To protect yourself and your content, however, you might want to register your site with the U.S. Copyright Office. Registration is voluntary and relatively simple—there's a small registration fee (about $35) and a few forms to fill out—but it provides you with legal recourse if you find that someone is infringing upon your copyright.

Registration isn't necessary to copyright your work, however, and it may not make sense for all net services, especially bloggers. Your work is copyrighted as soon as you publish it to your site, and you're free to place a notice on your site that it is copyright protected, whether you've registered it with the U.S. Copyright Office or not. The benefit to registering is that it will allow you to bring a lawsuit against someone for copyright infringement. The reason it doesn't make sense for many websites, though, is that you would have to repeatedly register (and pay filing fees) for all the new content you create. According to Copyright.gov, "copyrightable revisions to online works that are published on separate days *must each be registered individually,* with a separate application and filing fee."

The Copyright Office does have a provision for registering serial publications, such as newsletters or magazines, that are published online, but notes that an electronic journal, like a blog, doesn't fit into that category. According to Copyright.gov: "Group registration is not available for electronic journals published one article at a time because such works are not collective works."

If you do decide to register your website content with the U.S. Copyright Office—and the process does make sense for some net services—you can expect to receive your certificate of copyright four to five months after your forms are submitted and processed. Find out more at copyright.gov.

Business Insurance

Insurance is not just something you purchase to protect your home and your automobile. Your business is now—or it soon will be—one of your most important assets, and it, too, needs the protection of insurance. Don't wait to get business insurance; some

Stay on the Right Side of the Law

Don't assume your basic blog is exempt from the legal issues that affect the mainstream press. A newspaper can't publish libelous statements; neither can your blog. So before you begin writing, you should brush up on the liability issues that bloggers may face.

Perhaps the biggest legal issue bloggers can face is defamation. "Generally, defamation is a false and unprivileged statement of fact that is harmful to someone's reputation, and published 'with fault,' meaning as a result of negligence or malice," according to the Electronic Frontier Foundation's website (eff.org). Libel is written defamation; if the defamation is spoken, it's called slander.

Other legal issues that may affect bloggers include the use of someone else's intellectual property (including quotes you may publish and links to other sites) and public disclosure of private facts.

For more information, visit the EFF's *Legal Guide for Bloggers* at eff.org/bloggers/lg.

entrepreneurs put it off until they're turning a profit, thinking they don't need it yet. But you do.

Startup Basics covers the types of insurance that most small businesses will need, including workers' comp, general liability, auto insurance and property/casualty coverage. Not all of these apply to your net service—you're not likely to require auto insurance unless you're providing your employees with vehicles, for example—but most do.

- **General liability insurance** is especially important. This will cover your business assets if you are sued for any accidents or mishaps that cause bodily injury, property damage or personal injury. It also protects against advertising injury, which is considered to be damage from slander or false advertising. The "Cover Your Assets" chapter in *Startup Basics* offers more information on general liability insurance, including some of the exclusions it may have.

- **Errors and omissions (E&O)** is another type of insurance that many technology and consulting companies need; in fact, if you have investors or a board of directors, they may require it. E&O insurance, also referred to as professional liability insurance, protects you against any errors and omissions in the service that you deliver. It's specifically related to products and services delivered by a company. An SEM company may need E&O insurance to protect them against a client who decides that a downturn in their business is a result of erroneous advice given to them by the search engine marketer. While the contract you have in place with the client will provide some protection against such cases, E&O insurance is always a good idea.

- **Media liability** is a form of insurance that content providers—blogs and perhaps new media services—should consider. It protects your company against claims that may arise when you gather and communicate information to the public. Types of claims covered would include defamation, personal disparagement, and invasion or infringement, which includes public disclosure of private facts, unwarranted or wrongful publicity, or the use of names or likenesses for profit. Media liability insurance can be pricey; your annual premiums typically start at $2,500 to $3,500, and can escalate into a six-figure range. Deductibles also start around $10,000 and climb from there. Your premium and deductible will be determined by several factors, including the subject of your blog or website, your skill level as a writer (a journalist who has taken classes in media law, for example, may get a lower premium), and your expertise in the subject you're covering.

- **Data insurance**—also called "hacker insurance," "network risk insurance" or "network security insurance"—is a newer field. This is designed for companies, like net services, that deal in information. While traditional insurance policies protect assets like computers and equipment, this type of policy will protect you against the loss of information. This is especially important to consider if you collect and store information on your service's users, as some net services do. If that information were to fall into the hands of a hacker, a user could potentially sue you. This type of insurance could protect you.

Getting Outside Help

All this information may sound overwhelming, but help is available: You just have to ask—and you should. When in doubt, turn to a professional. It may seem expensive, but, most times, the expense can save you even more money down the road.

One of the professionals you might need to turn to for help is an insurance agent. Business insurance is a confusing field to navigate alone, and an experienced professional can help guide you. An insurance agent can explain what your insurance will and won't cover, how much coverage you need, and what types of insurance make sense for your business. Remember, though, that many insurance agents may not be familiar with your net service—even insurance agents well-versed in small-business needs may not fully understand your company. Ask others in your industry for recommendations on insurance agents they trust.

One professional every small business can benefit from is a lawyer. A lawyer can help with any variety of startup issues, including structuring your business; reviewing legal forms, such as partnership agreements, leases and contracts; advising you on liability issues; and filing patents, trademarks and copyrights. Don't wait until you're facing a lawsuit to hire an attorney; find one that you like well before that ever happens.

When hiring a lawyer, you should also look for someone familiar with small businesses and—if at all possible—with your industry. If you're planning on seeking venture capital funding, you'll definitely want an attorney familiar with the VC industry; finding a lawyer that the VC industry is familiar with would be an added bonus.

⚠ Beware!

Chances are, your small business needs a lawyer. But is one lawyer enough? Keep in mind that not every attorney can handlc all the legal needs your net service may face. A good attorney will know his limits and point you elsewhere when needed.

You likely won't need a full-time accountant on staff for quite a while, so it can be helpful to hire outside help in this area, too. Like a lawyer, your accountant can provide advice on what type of business structure you'd benefit from using; in fact, your accountant and your attorney may work closely together on these kinds of issues. An accountant also can set up your books and your accounting system to make sure you're properly paying employees and your taxes. An accountant can help with everything from tax preparation and financial reports to invoicing and payroll.

An accountant is not going to handle the day-to-day—or even the week-to-week—finances of your business. If you need that kind of help, you'll need to hire a bookkeeper or enlist the help of a bookkeeping service. A bookkeeper handles the systematic aspect of actually keeping your books, tracking how much money comes in and how much money goes back out. With the wide variety of accounting software packages available today, many small-business owners are completely capable of keeping their own books. But if you find you need help, hire a bookkeeper. Your financial records are too important to mess with.

All small-business owners will find they need the help of a professional at some point. As a general rule, if you think you need help, you do. Don't wait until it's too late to ask for it.

Getting
Financing

You're almost there. You have the idea for your business all hashed out. Your business plan is written. You're well-versed in your industry, and you have the competition all mapped out. Now it's time to raise some money. But where is that money going to come from?

The first place it's going to come from is you. That's right: You're the most important source of financing for your business.

▲

The "All in the Family" chapter of *Startup Basics* covers this in more detail, but you need to invest as much as you can of your own money in your business. How can you expect other people to invest in your business if you don't do so yourself?

The next place you can look for money is your friends and family. If you're looking for loans or financing from your friends, relatives and business associates, you need to treat them with the same respect you would give to a banker or a venture capitalist. You're not asking your dad for $50 to fill your car with gas; you need to schedule a meeting, present your business plan, and explain in detail exactly how you'll use their money to run your business. You should treat this loan just as formally as if it came from a bank: Put a loan agreement on paper and sign it.

Equity Financing

When you think of equity financing, you probably think of venture capitalists. But VCs are only one source of equity financing, and they're a scarce source at that. Equity financing involves giving up some of the control you have over your company; for this very reason, it's not for everyone.

Is Equity Financing Right for You?

Equity financing involves exchanging an ownership stake in your company for capital. Typically, the money will come from either VCs or private investors. The ownership stake you give up could be in the form of stock; alternatively, you could be forced to take on an active business partner. No matter how the details work out, you'll be giving up some of the control you have of the company. So you need to think long and hard about just how willing you are to turn your company over to someone else before you consider equity financing.

Rick Marini experienced this trade-off first hand when he founded Tickle. His company was in business for nine months before he accepted VC funds. "The earlier you take VC funding, the more equity you give up. The longer you can wait, the more you can prove out your business model, the more you'll be able to retain in equity," he says.

Your investors may take a very passive, hands-off role when it comes to the running of your company, but it's likely they'll insist on certain contract provisions.

Stat Fact
Venture capitalists invested $1.34 billion in Web 2.0 companies in 2007—an increase of 88 percent over the prior year, a recent survey by Dow Jones VentureSource reveals. While this shows that VC funding is on the rise, those numbers are slightly deceiving, as nearly $300 million of the money invested went to one company: Facebook.

These may allow them to make management changes under certain conditions or take complete control of your company should you fail to meet certain goals.

Giving up some control of your company isn't necessarily a bad thing. "Sometimes, especially if you have a big idea for a company, you may have no choice but to go to VCs," notes Marini. "And they may give you enough value to stomach the dilution."

Think of it this way: If you bring on equity investors, your ownership share of the company may drop to 10 percent by the time the company is sold or goes public. But those equity investors have helped drive the value of your company to $100 million. Without them, you'd own 100 percent of your company, but it may not be worth anything. Ten percent of $100 million is better than 100 percent of nothing.

One way to ensure your role within your company is to make yourself indispensable. If you can't easily be replaced, then you have a lot of leverage even though you may not control the business.

Venture Capital

OK, you've given it some thought and you're ready to hand over some control of your company. You think venture capital is right for you. Now comes the hard part: convincing the VCs that your company is right for them. Unfortunately, the era of VCs happily handing over forklifts of money to internet startups is over. Yes, there are still VC firms out there—quite a few, actually—but venture capital is more likely to be given to an established company with an already proven track record or to an entrepreneur with the same. VCs also like big ideas.

> **Bright Idea**
> If you were denied VC funds, refine your presentation and pitch again. Ask for feedback from the VCs who turned you down; if possible, find the partner who sponsored you and ask why you were turned down. You might be surprised at how candid the VCs will be with you.

"Venture capitalists are looking for the next Google," Marini says. "If you have a small idea that won't scale well, it might be a nice company for you to run, but VCs aren't the way to go."

Venture capitalists, obviously, are in business to make money. So they need to know that they can make money off your company. That means they're looking to invest in businesses that can go public or be acquired. If your company isn't likely to be acquired or have an IPO, then venture capital may not be a good fit for you.

Before the dotcom crash, internet companies were able to raise droves of cash though IPOs, but in today's market, that's less common. Investors aren't as willing to pour their money into a company just because it's an internet company—in fact, they may be scared away from investing in a company just because it's an internet company.

▲

California, Here We Come?

When you're looking for a VC firm, keep in mind that most of them will want the companies they invest in to be easily accessible. "Most VCs like to be able to drive to their portfolio companies or, at the very least, take a short flight," VentureSource's Jessica Canning notes.

You should also keep in mind that the majority of venture capital investment takes place in California, specifically in Silicon Valley, which is near the San Francisco Bay Area. "If you're looking for VCs, you'll find most of them on Sand Hill Road," Marini says. Sand Hill Road is in Menlo Park, California, in the heart of Silicon Valley.

Your greatest opportunity to gain VC funding is likely to be in this area and, should your proposal be accepted, the VCs will likely want your company to be based there. Marini knows this from personal experience: He moved his company from Cambridge, Massachusetts, to San Francisco right before the company landed VC funds.

According to Dow Jones VentureSource, the vast majority of Web 2.0 venture capital investments took place in this area in 2007. Of 178 total deals made with Web 2.0 companies in 2007, 72 of them—worth $721 million—took place in the Bay Area.

It's possible to find VC funds outside Silicon Valley—and you may face less competition in other areas, especially as a net services startup. New England was the second most popular location for landing VC funding on VentureSource's list, as it was home to 20 deals worth $158 million. Southern California came in third, with 14 deals valued at $115 million.

Still, if you have your heart—and your company's future—set on venture capital financing, you should give more than just a passing thought toward a Silicon Valley location.

"It's much harder for companies to go public now," says Jessica Canning, director of global research with Dow Jones VentureSource. "If you're targeting a small, niche market, it's going to be [especially] difficult to go public."

Today, instead of raising money through IPOs, the majority of VC-backed companies get acquired, Canning notes, so you should keep that in mind when writing your business plan and pitching your company to potential investors.

It's likely that your request for venture capital will initially be declined, but if you're serious about acquiring this type of funding, you shouldn't give up right away. "If you think about it, a venture capitalist says no about 99 percent of the time. As an entrepreneur, you're likely to be in that 99 percent," Marini says. "You should give it another shot. Don't stop because one venture capitalist said no."

Angel Investors

Getting financing from venture capitalists may be a long shot, but it's not your only option. There are plenty of other sources you can tap for equity financing—typically with far fewer strings attached. One source of private capital is an investment angel, someone who invests his or her money in an entrepreneurial company (unlike institutional venture capitalists, who invest other people's money).

Angels can be classified as affiliated or nonaffiliated. An affiliated angel is someone who has some sort of contact with you or your business but is not necessarily related to or acquainted with you. A nonaffiliated angel has no connection with you or your business.

Potential categories of angel investors include:

- **Professionals:** These include professional providers of services you use now—doctors, dentists, lawyers, accountants and so on. You know these people, so an appointment should be easy to arrange. Professionals usually have discretionary income available to invest in outside projects, and if they're not interested, they may be able to recommend a colleague who is.

- **Business associates:** These are people you come in contact with during the normal course of your business day. You should consider the vendors you work with on a regular basis, your customers, your employees and even your competitors, albeit those you don't directly compete with, as potential angel investors.

Nonaffiliated angels include professionals you don't know personally, managers and middle managers of companies who may be looking for side projects, and entrepreneurs who have been successful in their own businesses.

Approaching affiliated angels is simply a matter of making an appointment. But how do you find nonaffiliated angels? You might try advertising, networking with other entrepreneurs, and working with intermediaries, or "boutique investment firms," that focus on small financing deals. You can also research networks of angel investors online.

> ⚠ **Beware!**
> Not all angel investors are a good fit for you. Look for an investor who has experience in or can offer insight about your industry.

Keep in mind that not every angel investor is a good fit for your net service. Sure, the dentist down the street may have plenty of discretionary income to invest, but he may not know anything about your industry. Whenever possible, you should look for angels who are knowledgeable about your industry. Angels tend to be more involved in your business than VCs, and you'll want to use their expertise to your advantage.

Acquiring Angel Funds

Angel investors may have a reputation as being easier to convince than venture capitalists, but that's not always true. It *is* true that angels may be motivated as much by the enjoyment of helping a young business succeed as they are by big ROIs. Angels are more likely than venture capitalists to be persuaded by an entrepreneur's drive to succeed, persistence and mental discipline. Keep in mind, however, that angels look for many of the same things that professional venture capitalists look for. When pitching your business plan to one, pitch it as you would to a VC firm. Things they consider include:

- **Strong management:** Does your management team have a track record of experience and success?

- **Proprietary strength:** Proprietary doesn't necessarily mean you own the patents, copyrights or trademarks on your service. It just means that your service should be unusual enough to grab the attention of your clients or consumers.

- **Window of opportunity:** Investors look for a window of opportunity when your company can be the first in a market and grab the lion's share of business before others.

- **Market potential:** Investors prefer businesses with strong market potential. This means a net service that could attract anyone who uses the internet stands a better chance than one targeted only at the folks in your small town.

- **ROI:** Most angels will expect a return of 20 to 25 percent over five years. However, they may accept a lower rate of return if your business has lower risk.

That's why it's important that your business plan convey a good sense of your background, experience and drive. Your business plan also should address the concerns just mentioned and spell out the financing you expect to receive from startup to maturity.

What if your plan is rejected? Ask for feedback, and ask the angel if he or she knows someone else your business plan might appeal to. If your plan is accepted, you have some negotiating to do. Be sure to spell out all the terms of the investment in a written agreement; get your lawyer's assistance here. How long will the investment last? How will return be calculated? How will the investment be cashed out? Detail the amount of involvement each angel will have in the business and how the investment will be legalized.

Debt Financing

You may have decided that equity financing is not for you. This is an absolutely fair assessment to make. And in many cases—if you're starting a small blogging business, for example—it might never be an option to consider. So what do you do if you or your business isn't a good fit for equity financing but you still need funding?

Debt financing, which involves receiving money in the form of a loan that you have to repay, is another alternative. The "Fed Funds" chapter in *Startup Basics* includes information on obtaining government loans. Government loans aren't the only kind of loans available, though. You can also turn to banks, commercial lenders and even personal credit cards.

> ## Smart Tip
>
> **Tip...**
>
> Most businesses can benefit from establishing a line of credit, even if you don't need it right away. It can protect your business from emergencies and stalled cash flow.

There are many types of loans available, and you don't have to know exactly which type you'd like before you approach a lender; he or she can help you decide what type of financing is best for your needs. Still, you should be familiar with the different types of loans so you can understand what your lender is offering. Keep in mind that the same type of loan may come with different terms at different banks.

- **Line-of-credit loans:** This is a short-term loan that extends the cash available in your business's checking account to the upper limit of the loan contract. Every bank has its own method of funding, but, essentially, an amount is transferred to the business's checking account to cover checks. The business pays the interest on the actual amount advanced; the principal is paid off at your convenience. Bankers may also call this a revolving line of credit.

- **Installment loans:** These loans are paid back with equal monthly payments covering both principal and interest. Installment loans may be written to meet all types of business needs. You receive the full amount when the contract is signed, and the interest is calculated from that date to the final day of the loan. You can repay an installment loan before its final date with no penalty.

- **Balloon loans:** Typically written under another name, a balloon loan can be identified by these characteristics: The full amount is received when the contract is signed, but only the interest is paid off during the life of the loan. A lump sum—or "balloon"—payment of the principal is due on the final day. A balloon loan may work for your net service if you must wait until a specific date before receiving payment from your client.

A loan can be secured or unsecured. An unsecured loan—which can be very difficult to obtain as a startup—has no collateral pledged as a secondary payment source should you default on the loan. A secured loan requires some kind of collateral but may have a lower interest rate than an unsecured loan.

Banks all over the country write loans, especially installment and balloon loans, under a myriad of names. They include term loans; second mortgages (where real estate is used to secure a loan); inventory loans and equipment loans (for the purchase of, and secured by, inventory or equipment); accounts receivable loans (secured by your outstanding accounts); personal loans (where your signature and personal collateral guarantee the loan, which you lend to your business); guaranteed loans (in which a third party—an investor, spouse or the SBA—guarantees repayment); or commercial loans (a general term for a bank's standard loan for small businesses).

Sources of Debt Financing

When seeking debt financing, where do you begin? Carefully choosing the lenders you target can increase your odds of success. Here's a look at various loan sources and what you should know about each.

More and more major banks are offering special services and programs for small businesses; others have streamlined their loan paperwork and approval process to get loans to entrepreneurs faster. While this may sound like good news for entrepreneurs like you, it also means that—more than ever—loan approval is based solely on numbers and scores on standardized ratings systems.

Given the challenges of working with a big bank, many entrepreneurs are taking a different tack: They're looking to their community banks. Here, "relationship banking" is more likely to come into play. Community banks have the ability to be more flexible, don't have a bureaucracy to deal with, and are more apt to make characters loans. Don't get the idea that obtaining a loan from a community bank is a snap, however. You'll still have to meet credit and collateral requirements just as you would at a larger institution.

> **! Beware!**
> Even though a bank may offer a loan program targeted toward small business, that doesn't mean those funds will be easier to obtain.

Boost your chances of getting a loan by finding a lender whose experience matches your needs. Keep in mind that many community bankers—and many bankers at larger institutions as well—may look at your idea for a net service with a skeptical eye. Internet startups often get a bad rap. But if you can find someone who is knowledgeable about your industry, and you can show them how well you've done your homework, your chances for successfully obtaining a loan increase greatly. Ask experts and others in your industry for leads on banks; putting in the work to find the right lender can pay off.

Banks aren't your only option when seeking a loan. Consider a nonbank commercial lender or commercial finance company. Many of these firms have expanded their focus on small businesses. While commercial finance companies require much of the same information that any loan provider will expect—your business plan, detailed financial statements and cash flow projections—the loans may be easier to obtain.

Borrowing Money the Web 2.0 Way

Banks and credit cards aren't your only options for debt financing. If you're looking for a loan to get your net service up and running, why not turn to another net service? Companies like Prosper and Lending Club offer social lending networks that connect individuals and small businesses that need money with people who have money to lend.

Prosper (prosper.com) and Lending Club (lendingclub.com) work in a similar manner: They let people with extra money lend that money to individuals and businesses that need it. Lenders make a profit through the interest charged on the loan. Borrowers fill out applications on the site and are matched with lenders who fit their needs. Money is not passed directly from lender to borrower; both companies handle all the money management themselves.

The interest rates you'll pay on loans from these types of services vary, so you'll want to make sure they're for you before you sign up. But if you're in need of funding, they offer a unique way to find it.

The downside: These loans typically come with a higher interest rate than you'd find elsewhere. For more information on finding a lender, visit the website of the Commercial Finance Association at cfa.com.

Using your personal credit cards is another—albeit very risky—way of obtaining financing. The obvious drawback is the high interest rates, which tend to climb even higher if you use the cards for cash advances rather than purchases. Credit card financing is an option that's best for very small businesses; if you're starting up an individual web design firm or a small blogging business, a credit card may provide all the financing you'll ever

> **Bright Idea**
> If you see the interest rate on your credit card creeping up, try to negotiate a lower rate. Many card issuers will extend this courtesy to customers who call.

need. And if you're good at juggling payments and are confident you can pay the money back quickly, this can be the easiest way to go.

Should you decide to go this route, you should always seek out the lowest interest rate you can find and transfer balances when introductory rates climb. You may be able to get the card issuer to extend the low introductory rate by negotiating with them over the phone. You must also pay more than the minimum due. This may sound like common sense, but you should always pay off your balance whenever you can. This means you should never charge more than you'll be able to pay off within a reasonable time frame.

Planning Your Exit Strategy

It may seem a bit early to think about selling your business—after all, you're still in the planning stages—but if you're looking for financing, you need to keep your exit strategy in mind. And for many internet companies, that exit strategy is an acquisition. No matter how much of your blood, sweat and tears you've poured into your net service, there's always a time to think about selling. But how do you know if you're ready?

Before the time comes when you—or your investors—are contemplating a sale that would buy you out and leave you completely uninvolved with the business, you should think hard about several factors so you can be prepared. (Though if your investors are making the decision, you may not have much say in the matter. But we warned you about this already.)

One factor to consider is whether or not you're ready to give up the business you've worked so hard to grow. Can you handle turning it over to someone else, and will you know what to do with yourself once you have? Maybe you already have an idea for another company you'd like to start; that's a pretty good sign that you're ready to sell.

You also have to consider the impact on your clients. How much interaction do you—and any of your partners or employees who may not be around after the sale—have with them? What will it mean to your clients if you're no longer the face of the company? Will they still get the service and support they're used to? What becomes of the relationships they've developed with you? While you can't let guilt sway you, you should take your clients into account.

You also need to be aware of the overall health of your business. How much is it worth—not just to you but to a purchaser? Are there any problems—legal, financial or otherwise—that may scare away a buyer? Being honest about these issues upfront will make the entire process much easier.

After your business has been sold, you may still be involved in it, and, in some cases, this can be a boon for entrepreneurs. Google, after all, has snapped up many a small business. It acquired blogging company Pyra Labs; video-sharing site YouTube; 2Web Technologies, an online spreadsheet provider; DoubleClick, an online advertising company; and FeedBurner, a company that offers a variety of products for accessing web feeds. And those are just a few of Google's numerous acquisitions.

Being acquired by Google—or Yahoo! or another big-name internet company—is the goal of many entrepreneurs. Your product

> **Fun Fact**
> At 24, Mark Zuckerberg, the founder and CEO of Facebook, is the youngest self-made billionaire to land on *Forbes's* list. His fortune is estimated at $1.5 billion.

reaches a much wider audience and you (often) get the benefit of working for Google or Yahoo!—and those are the kinds of companies people like to work for. That is, of course, assuming they decide to keep you on board. There are downsides, however— the primary one being the loss of control over your company and its products. Sure, your online spreadsheet may reach billions of users now that Google owns it, but it may look far different than the product you worked so hard to build. In addition, the name you gave your product and your company likely is long gone.

And acquisition isn't for everyone. Yahoo!, for example, attempted to acquire the social networking site Facebook for as much as $1 billion in 2006, but the company's founder and CEO Mark Zuckerberg—who was only 22 years old at the time—turned down the offer. A year later, his company was valued at more than $15 billion, and he was listed on the *Forbes* list of billionaires—and he still retained control over his company. Turning down an acquisition—especially one with that many zeroes attached to it—is a risk, to be sure. Who's to say your company, even if it is Facebook, will retain its value? What happens to you and your employees if it doesn't? These are all factors to consider when faced with a purchase offer.

Selling your business will be much easier if you've planned for it from the start. If you've received venture capital funding or other types of investments, you may have been forced to put these types of plans on paper. Remember that selling your company can take time; in some cases, it may take longer than it took to get your business up and running. For more tips and information on selling a small business, visit the SBA's website at sba.gov.

Getting to
Work

Now that you've settled many of the details of your business, you need to find a place to work. Let's start at the most basic level: Do you need to rent office space, or can you work from home?

Should You Work from Home?

You're not selling goods to consumers or other businesses, so you don't need a physical storefront. You likely don't have much in the way of inventory or supplies on hand, so you don't need a place to store them. Unless you have clients or investors who want to visit your place of business, chances are very good that you can start your business from home. And in many cases, you won't need to work from anywhere else throughout the life of your business. Bloggers, freelance web designers and search engine marketers who work as consultants are among those who may never need to find office space.

"A lot of consultants do have their own office, but a lot work out of their home offices. It really depends on what you prefer. The majority of your work is done over the phone and the internet—this is why you need a good online presence and reputation," SEM consultant Todd Mailcoat says.

Many small businesses start out as homebased businesses that eventually grow to the point where they need office space. That's what Robert Cavilla and his partner did when they founded UpWord SEM in Boston.

"There's no real reason to have office space unless you have employees or you want your clients to visit you. Realistically, most of the time you visit them," Cavilla says. "Once we realized we needed employees, we realized we needed office space."

While it's possible that your business will hire only virtual employees (such as freelancers and contractors who work from their own homes), you should have an office if you're hiring people who will work in your physical location. It gives a much more professional image and shows that you have a commitment to your business. Having employees in your home—and their cars parked out front—can also lead to zoning difficulties.

The Siren Call of Silicon Valley

If you do decide to rent office space, one of the most important decisions you'll make is about the location. As a net service, your business is virtual—that means it can be located almost anywhere. An SEM firm in Florida can work with clients in Indiana, while a website designer in Texas can build sites for an Oregon company. As long as you have internet access, your business can be up and running anywhere.

"I have a laptop and a cell phone. That's what I work off on a daily basis. I'm in vagabond mode. I work from wherever I feel like being," Mailcoat says.

That means it's very possible to start your net service from wherever it is you live now—in most cases. But some net services, especially new media services, may find they need to be located where they can attract the attention of investors and recruit the best employees.

In the previous chapter, we explained that investors—especially venture capitalists—like their portfolio companies to be easily accessible to them. As most VC firms are located in Silicon Valley, so, too, are many tech companies. Naturally, locating your company in Northern California has its advantages and disadvantages.

Rick Marini, a New Hampshire native, started Tickle (then called eMode) in Cambridge, Massachusetts. Within the first year, though, he and his partner moved the company to San Francisco for several reasons. One was to be closer to prominent venture capital firms (and the company did obtain funding from a VC located there). But that wasn't the only reason—in fact, it wasn't even the primary reason. "The number-one reason was the talent pool. There were great engineers [in Cambridge] from MIT, but we needed more people. We needed content people, marketing people. There's a much broader and deeper pool of people in Silicon Valley," Marini says.

Another reason? Silicon Valley is to internet entrepreneurs what Washington, DC is to politicians, says Marini. "Everyone speaks the same language. You hear people talking about it at bars and cocktail parties. If you have the availability, Silicon Valley is the place to be," Marini notes.

Of course, running your business in "the place to be" is expensive. Office rents and employee salaries are likely to be higher than what you'd find elsewhere (though the same is true of many large cities). You're also going to face steeper competition to attract and retain employees. What's going to convince someone to work for you if they can work for Google instead? (We'll offer some tips on how to attract employees in Chapter 12.)

Remember that Silicon Valley isn't your only choice. But it's definitely a place to consider.

Choosing Office Space

Whether you decide to base your company in Silicon Valley or not, there are some basic things to keep in mind when selecting office space. In years past, the offices of dotcom startups were lavish and outlandish. You don't have to—and you shouldn't—go overboard, but you do want to select a location and create an atmosphere that will appeal to your clients and employees.

When looking at potential office space, consider these criteria:

- **Commuting:** You and your employees will be traveling to and from your office on a daily basis. How far is it located from where you—and the majority of your employees—live? Is it easily accessible from a major highway? Chances are you won't be able to find a location that offers an easy commute for everyone, but consider nearby traffic before signing a lease.

- **Cubicles vs. offices:** Will your employees spend a lot of their time collaborating with one another, or will they be talking to clients on the phone? This may determine whether or not you select a space that has mainly offices or a more open space with cubicles. You may also need a good-sized meeting room to allow for team meetings.

- **Image:** If you expect clients and investors to visit, consider what kind of image the space projects. Does it look polished and professional? You're likely to have an easier time attracting employees if your office space impresses them. And while your office doesn't have to be so laid-back that employees are riding around on scooters, you do want to think about what kind of environment you're creating. If you're looking to attract and retain young employees, consider whether the environment will appeal to them.

- **Amenities:** Do you need a kitchen or a break room? Is there a sandwich shop located in the building or nearby? You don't want your employees—or yourself—starving because there's no place to buy a snack.

- **Adaptability:** You may have five employees right now, but in a year, you may need to add 10 more. Can your office space accommodate that many people? Is there additional space available in the building should you require more? Can you reallocate the current space if needed?

> **! Beware!**
> Most office leases last between three and five years; one-year leases can be difficult to find. Make sure you'll need the space for that long—and that the space will fit your needs for that time period, too.

These are just a few of the things you should think about before signing your lease. Keep in mind that the market for office space has changed drastically in recent years; many cities have vacancy rates that are much higher than they were eight or nine years ago. This could mean that bargains or subleases may be easier to find. Carefully weigh all your options and make sure that you—and your lawyer—read the fine print before you sign anything.

Outfitting Your Office

Now that you've found the perfect place to work, let's talk about getting it all set up. What kind of equipment do you need to run your net service?

The Basics

Whether you're working out of your home or leasing office space, you're obviously going to need desks and chairs for all your employees. Some office lease agreements will include furniture, but some won't, so you need to read the fine print and find out

Making the Grade

Office space is typically classified as Class A, B or C. While these letters may mean little to you initially, they can drastically affect the price you'll pay—and the quality of the space you'll find. Here's a brief overview of what they mean.

- **Class A,** not surprisingly, is used to label office space that's considered to be the highest quality. A Class A building typically features a desirable location, an attractive design, newer construction, amenities for tenants and—of course—the highest price tag.
- **Class B** office space may be located in older, smaller buildings than Class A space. It also may be in a newer, nicer building that's in a location that's not optimal.
- **Class C** buildings are typically older (upward of 25 years old) and are not considered desirable. They may be located above retail stores in some neighborhoods.

All these ratings are subjective; there's no governing body that classifies office real estate. Just as you would when buying a property for your personal use, you should visit your potential office space in person to judge for yourself.

what you'll need to supply. If you're working from home, you'll likely buy your own furniture (new or used); if you're leasing an office, you may also consider leasing your furniture. Whatever you decide to do, you should make sure that the desks and chairs you choose are comfortable—you'll be spending a lot of time in them!

You should also keep in mind that the furniture you choose will go a long way in establishing the image of your company. That doesn't mean you have to buy the most expensive desk chairs around; it's simply another thing to consider when making your purchase. If clients will be visiting your office, think about how your furnishings will look to them.

You'll also need phones and phone service; even if you're working out of your home, you need a dedicated phone line for your business. Additionally, you may want to consider a copier and a fax machine, depending on the nature of your net service. Faxing may seem antiquated in your virtual online environment, but a fax machine could prove handy. If you don't plan on sending or receiving many faxes, you may find you can get by without one or you may be able to opt for a service like eFax (efax.com), which allows you to send and receive faxes online.

Beyond that, you'll need basic office supplies, such as pens, paper, paper clips, staplers, Post-it notes and file folders. You don't need to go crazy purchasing these supplies—if you're working out of a home office, you likely have plenty of them lying around. You shouldn't need to spend more than a few hundred dollars on office supplies to outfit your office at startup.

Computer Hardware

In each of the chapters on the specific types of net services, we discussed the hardware and software you'll need to start that type of business. But there are some types of hardware and software that every net service needs.

Smart Tip

Tip...

When creating your home office, try to create a barrier between it and the rest of your house. Whether you locate it in the farthest corner of your house or simply make sure it has a door that you can close, you'll appreciate the separation.

You'll need desktop or laptop computers for each employee. In general, desktops tend to provide more power and capacity for less money than you'd spend on a comparable laptop. Desktops can also be more easily expanded and upgraded than laptops. If you or your employees will be traveling to client offices or trade shows and conferences, however, a laptop computer may make more sense. A laptop also gives you the opportunity to work from home or remotely should you require it.

Another option for mobile access is a smart phone. Devices like RIM's BlackBerrys, Apple's iPhone, and Windows Mobile-based phones like the Samsung BlackJack let you access your e-mail while you're away from the office. This can be a great way to respond to client inquiries quickly. Phones that run Windows Mobile also allow you to access and edit Microsoft Office documents—as long as you can stand using the small keyboard and screen provided.

Beware!
Your office lease may include desks but not chairs. Make sure you know what furniture you need to supply so you don't have employees sitting on the floor waiting for the chairs to arrive.

Some net services will require servers to host applications and websites and to store your data, such as customer information. You may also want a server in your office to provide a central storage space for files, making it easier for employees to collaborate. Typically, this type of server is referred to as a file server.

Purchasing a server can be daunting even for the most technologically savvy entrepreneurs. While any PC could technically be used as a server, you should—if possible—purchase a dedicated server system. Buy a server with as much memory, storage and processing power as you think you'll need a year from now. Your server needs may be minimal today, but that's likely to change, so you should future-proof your investment as best you can. Educate yourself before making your purchase so you can feel confident in your decision.

Software

When it comes to software, everyone will need a basic office or productivity suite. Microsoft's ubiquitous Office suite may be the first one that comes to mind, but it's expensive: The list price for Office Small Business is $450. Using the suite can make sense, however, as most of your employees and clients will be familiar with the software, and the files and documents you create can easily be opened by anyone else who is using the applications. There are other alternatives, though, and many of them are compatible with Microsoft Office. Corel, IBM and OpenOffice offer productivity suites that are much cheaper than Microsoft Office (in some cases, they're free).

Serving Up the Basics

Confused about servers? You're not alone. Here's a crash course in the basics.

Servers are computers designed to provide common access to their contents. Those contents may be files, a website, an e-mail system or applications. Servers are connected to your employees' computers via your company's network or the internet.

Servers have both hardware components (the computing box itself) and software components (the operating system and applications that it runs). How you plan to use the server will determine both your hardware and software needs. If you plan to use it for basic file sharing among a very small work group, for example, you may be able to purchase low-end server hardware and run a desktop version of Windows XP or Vista on it; these operating systems include built-in file-sharing features.

As your needs grow, so, too, will your server requirements. If you plan to use your server to host a database containing all your clients' personal data, you'll need to select a secure database application that can hold your information. Then you'll need to find a dedicated server operating system, such as Windows Small Business Server or one of the various versions of Linux. These operating systems will require a more robust piece of hardware on which to run, so you'll have to take their system requirements into account when making your purchase.

Server hardware is available in various forms, including PC-like towers or smaller rack-mounted models, which can fit on shelves.

It may sound confusing, but help is available. Look for a reseller, like CDW (cdw.com) or PC Connection (pcconnection.com) that can offer you a complete server package, including the hardware, operating system and applications you need. They can guide you through the entire process.

You'll also need security software. This is a must. You can opt for a complete suite, like those offered by McAfee, Symantec, Kaspersky and Trend Micro, which typically offer anti-virus, anti-spyware, a firewall and internet security tools. You must use security software to protect individual desktops, laptops and servers. A virus or spyware could wreak havoc on your network, and that's a risk you don't want to take.

> **Beware!**
> If you're considering storing confidential company information or client data on a laptop, be very careful. Laptops can easily be lost or stolen, and losing your sensitive data can prove even more costly than losing the hardware itself.

Accounting software is another must-have. We'll offer some tips for managing your finances in Chapter 11, and an accounting package can simplify those tasks. As a solo practitioner, you may be able to use an application like Quicken Home & Business, which manages both your personal and business finances. As your company grows, you'll likely have to opt for a business-only package, like those offered by Intuit and Peachtree.

Other types of software you may want to consider include a contact management or CRM tool for maintaining client lists and managing client relationships; project management or collaboration software, for tracking individual or group projects; business plan software, for help writing your business plan; and a database application for housing data. For more information on specific software for your business, read *Entrepreneur* magazine's "Complete Guide to Software" at entrepreneur.com/software.

Making
Money

At last, it's time to talk about the fun stuff: Money—specifically, where it will all come from. In some cases, money will come to you directly from your clients. If you're launching a website design company or an SEM firm, you'll (eventually) be charging clients for your services. But how will you generate revenue if you're launching a free blog or new media service? You have several options, from selling advertising space to offering subscriptions. For the purposes of this chapter, we're going to discuss the services with paying clients—website design and SEM—and then tackle the free services—blogs and new media services.

Web Design and SEM

Earlier in this book, we mentioned that you shouldn't charge for your website design services until you're certain the service you're providing is worth paying for. A similar argument was made for starting an SEM business: You must prove yourself and practice your skills before taking on paying clients.

Once you've made the decision that it's time to charge, however, you have a bigger question in front of you: How much? If you charge too little, you may not make enough to support yourself. You may also give your clients the impression that your services aren't very good. If you charge too much, however, you risk scaring away potential clients. It's a fine line.

Pricing Your Services: Website Design

One way to determine how much to charge is to figure out how much you need to make—or would like to make—as an annual salary. You can also use online salary services to find out the average salary for a web designer with a certain amount of experience. Payscale.com, for example, says that the average salary for a web designer with five to nine years of experience is $49,014. For our purposes, we'll say you're aiming to make an annual salary of $50,000.

To figure out how much you should charge, you need to do some math. First, you'll need to figure out how many billable hours you can work. Remember when we discussed the average day in the life of a web designer back in Chapter 2? James Paden, the web designer and owner of the Indianapolis-based Xemion web design directory, estimated that on a good day, he could spend a maximum of five hours on billable work. If that's the case for you, you can expect to work 25 billable hours in a good week; the rest of your time will likely be spent on the administrative tasks and day-to-day work of actually running your business.

If you can bill 25 hours per week, and you can work 50 weeks per year (we'll give you two weeks off for good behavior), that's 1,250 billable hours per year. To make $50,000 per year (before taxes and paying any of your bills), you need to charge $40 per hour.

Remember, that's a low estimate; many web designers actually charge upwards of $75

Stat Fact
The average salary for a website designer with one to four years of experience is $39,000, according to Payscale.com.

to $150 per hour. According to our formula, a rate of $40 per hour will result in a salary of $50,000, but that's before paying any utilities or overhead costs. So if you expect to pay rent on office space, you need to figure out how that will affect your bottom line. You should also consider the costs of your insurance, office supplies and all the other expenses you'll incur throughout the year. It also assumes you'll be able to find enough work to keep you occupied for 1,250 hours per year. Now you may understand why $40 per hour is a low estimate.

Now that we've walked you through one method of setting an hourly rate, we should point out that one of the biggest debates in this industry is whether or not to charge by the hour. Many web designers prefer to use a project fee. This has a couple of benefits: First, it gives your client the security of knowing their total charges upfront. Second, it gives you the added motivation to complete the project faster—and hence, actually raise your own hourly rate.

So how do you figure out what to charge on a project basis? One option is to charge per element. You can, for instance, charge per page or per design element (such as a graphic or a button), or use a flat rate for a site. Most designers, though, use another formula. Paden, for example, says he typically estimates how long a project will take him to complete, and then multiplies that by the figure he uses as his hourly rate. He presents the total to his client as the project fee, noting the estimated amount of time he expects to spend on the project.

You'll need to be upfront with your clients about exactly what that project fee includes, though. "If I get a client who is changing their mind too many times, asking me to redo too many things, I will usually sit down with them and explain the situation," says Paden. "I tell them that I estimated a certain amount of hours for their project, and that if it's going to go beyond that, the fee will go up. Most clients are very understanding."

The contract you give your clients before agreeing to any project should stipulate the terms. Spell out exactly how many revisions you'll offer and what the additional charge will be for any revisions beyond the agreed-upon number.

As you gain more experience and clients, you shouldn't be afraid to raise your rates, and, in fact, you may find that you need to in order to make the same amount of money. The more clients you have, the more time you may need to spend on non-billable tasks for those clients. You'll be handling more sales inquiries and customer support requests, so the hours you have available to work on actual projects will decrease. From time to time, you should evaluate your skills, your list of clients and your lifestyle, and then consider if your hourly rate needs to be adjusted.

Pricing Your Services: SEM

How you charge (and how much you charge) for your SEM services will vary depending on the actual services you offer. A consultant who provides advice and strategic guidance for his or her clients may charge by the hour, for example. An agency, on the other hand, may charge a flat, or project, fee for ongoing SEO services. For SEM (or "paid search") projects, the fee is typically a percentage of what the client spends.

As a consultant, how much can you charge? "I've struggled with this," says Todd Mailcoat, the SEM consultant from Troy, New York. "I'm almost embarrassed to admit it, but I charge $500 an hour," he says.

His hourly rate is based on several factors, he says. "I realize how much I value my time, and I know what kind of return I am making for my clients. I know that I am doubling, tripling, even quadrupling the amount of money they're making."

The rate is also based on the fact that much of his work, just like that of a web designer, is not billable. He spends much of his time researching the always evolving SEO field, practicing his skills on his own websites and, of course, handling the administrative tasks of running his business. All this nonbillable work is factored into the rate he charges when actually working on a billable project.

Of course, you won't be able to start out charging $500 per hour; you'll need to put in your time and pay your dues to build your expertise. According to Rand Fishkin, CEO of SEOMoz.org, average rates for entry-level consultants start at about $40 to $50 per hour, then climb to $100 to $200 per hour for mid-tier consultants. High-demand consultants like Mailcoat can charge $300 to $500 per hour and more, Fishkin says.

One way to increase your rate is to follow the model that Mailcoat used when he first started out as a web designer. "I started charging $25 to $50 an hour. As soon as I felt comfortable with my work, I doubled the rate for new clients. I had to believe I was providing that level of value."

SEM agencies charge for their services in a variety of ways. Some charge per hour for consulting services, while others charge a project-based fee for work that may include such components as a site review, keyword research and advice for implementing the suggested changes. Other agencies will charge a monthly retainer for ongoing work. Some agencies use a combination of all of the above, tailoring their pricing schemes for the work their clients request.

The most common ways SEO firms charge, according to Fishkin, are hourly fees, project-based fees, individual services for a set price (such as a directory-submis-

Smart Tip

If you're billing your clients on an hourly basis, you need to keep detailed records of the hours you work. Look for a software application or a service, like QuickBooks Time Tracker or Toggl.com, to help make the process easier.

sion service), profit sharing (in which the SEO firm takes a percentage of revenues made through the website they're optimizing), monthly retainers, pay for rankings (in which clients pay you based on which page of search engine results they attain), and pay for traffic (in which you get paid based on how much traffic your clients get).

Some of these methods are risky—the profit sharing and the pay-for-performance methods especially can be challenging and don't always end up working out in your favor. You should carefully weigh the pros and cons of any method before deciding which one works best for you.

How you charge is one thing; how *much* you can charge is another. One of the biggest factors that will affect this, of course, is your experience and reputation in the industry. In the chart on page 126, Fishkin estimates the range of fees that SEOs can charge.

As you can see, the fees vary greatly. In general, you should never charge less than you think your services are worth, but never charge so much that you feel as though your clients aren't getting their money's worth.

Fees for paid search services, also called PPC or pay-per-click, are typically set up differently. One of the most common pricing models is for the SEM provider to take a percentage—anywhere from 5 to 15 percent—of the client's "media spend." The industry average is typically 10 to 15 percent, but a firm just starting out may only be able to charge 5 percent as their management fee, notes UpWord SEM's Robert Cavilla.

To make it worth the time they invest, some SEM firms require clients to spend a minimum monthly amount or may charge an initial setup fee to begin the campaign. After all, if your client is spending $1,000 a month, your take of that would only be $150, even if you were charging 15 percent as a management fee.

Other PPC providers charge by the hour, taking into account the size of the campaign and the number of keywords they're targeting for their clients. Just like the fees charged by SEO consultants, these hourly rates can range greatly but typically will top out at $150 to $200 per hour.

Billing Your Clients

Most website designers take a deposit before beginning a project; the industry average is 50 percent, with the balance due upon successful completion of the project. (As you can see, even if you're charging on an hourly basis, you'll need to estimate a total for a project before you begin.) Some designers will take a smaller initial deposit but

SEO Fee Range

Service	Low End	Mid Range	High End
Site Review & Consulting	$500	$2,500	$10,000
Hands-on Editing of Page/Code	$2,000	$10,000	$50,000
Manual Link-Building Campaign	$500	$5,000	$20,000
One-Day SEO Training Seminar	$750	$4,000	$12,000
Keyword Research Package	$100	$500	$2,000
Viral Content Development & Mktg	$1,000	$7,500	$20,000
Web Design, Development & Mktg	$5,000	$25,000	$100,000+
Monthly Retainer for Ongoing SEO	$2,500	$7,500	$20,000+

Source: Rand Fishkin, SEOMoz.org

require more frequent, smaller payments throughout the project, perhaps when key stages are completed.

If the fee involved is very large, Paden says he may divide it into three payments: an initial deposit, another payment in the middle of the project, and the balance due when it's completed. Or, if he's dealing with a long-time customer, he may forego the upfront fee and collect the entire fee upon completion.

Billing for SEM services is similar but will vary depending, of course, on the pricing model you choose. Most firms bill their clients monthly, whether they're charging a project fee, an hourly fee or a monthly retainer. Some firms ask for a deposit up front, but Cavilla notes that you may have a hard time getting your clients to agree to this when you're just starting out.

Smart Tip

Tip...

Even if you're working as a sole proprietor, you should always ask that payments be made to your business name, not to you personally.

However you decide to bill your clients, you need to send invoices. You can generate your own invoices, either as Word documents or PDFs, which spell out the payment due and the terms. However, it may be easier to use a software application—either an accounting package for managing your business finances that includes an invoicing feature or a dedicated invoicing solution—that will generate them for you. You can send invoices by e-mail or snail mail, but you want to make sure you keep detailed records of when and how you send them. You never want a client to be able to say they didn't receive your bill.

Accepting Payment

The most common way to accept payment from clients is to have a check written to your business's account. When first starting out, some freelancers will accept checks written to them personally, but it's always a good idea to use a separate business checking account for all your business-related needs.

Most SEM and web design agencies accept credit cards; many individuals who work as freelancers or consultants are able to do so through online payment services like PayPal. You can sign up for an account on paypal.com, and the payments that your clients make via credit card will be deposited into your PayPal account. You can then transfer the funds from PayPal to your bank account. Keep in mind, however, that PayPal charges a fee; typical fees are about 2 to 3 percent of the transaction amount.

Some larger firms and consultancies may prefer to use a payment service other than PayPal in order to project a more professional image; other options include ProPay (propay.com) and checkfree.com. The business accounting application you use also may help you accept credit cards: Intuit, for example, offers a "Merchant Service" for its Quicken application that allows you to accept credit-card payments. It costs $13 per month.

New Media Service and Blogging Business

Unlike a website design firm or an SEM business, your new media service or blog likely won't have a list of clients to charge. You won't be sending out monthly invoices and collecting payments. But that doesn't mean there won't be money coming in. One of the most common ways free web services generate revenue is through advertising.

Before you can even think about making money from advertisements, however, you need to focus on growing the audience for your new media service or blog. "Focus on your content first," advises Tickle.com's Rick Marini. "Most advertisers don't care about you until you have enough eyeballs on your site anyway. Until you

▲

The PayPal Myth

Once you've signed up for a PayPal account and realize how easy it is to accept payments via credit card, you may think you've found nirvana. But you should keep in mind that PayPal is not a bank and doesn't offer many of the protections you might be used to getting from a financial institution.

PayPal, for example, offers a "seller protection policy" that's designed to protect people who use the service to make payments—people like your clients. This is obviously a good thing if those people are honest; unfortunately, not everyone is. Many online message boards and forums used by independent web designers to share information tell stories of freelancers who were stiffed on payments because their clients falsely reported to PayPal that they had not received the services they'd paid for.

In these instances, PayPal automatically deducts the fee from the account of the freelancer—you—and returns the money to the client. This can happen even when the full service has been delivered. Should this happen to you, PayPal allows you to appeal, but the burden of proof will lie on you. It will take time you don't have to make your case, and you might never get your money back.

Also keep in mind that should PayPal suffer an outage, the funds in your account may be inaccessible. And should the service—and your account—get hacked, you may lose all your money. PayPal is not a bank and is not FDIC-insured.

We're not saying you shouldn't use PayPal: it's a very handy, affordable service. But if you do, make sure you transfer the funds in your account to your bank account often. And be wary of its seller protection policy; it can work against you.

get enough traffic, you're only going to attract remnant advertisers, the bottom of the barrel. When you're first starting out, you don't want to have bad ads that will give people a reason to navigate away from your site."

Rob May, a blogger who launched—and eventually sold—BusinessPundit.com, tells a similar story. When he first began displaying advertising from Google AdSense, he made a whopping $23. "It wasn't even worth it," he says. "I took the ads off."

⚠ Beware!

When you begin accepting ads, watch where you place them. Don't waste good content space on ads.

Advertising

Once you've established enough of an audience to make it worthwhile to display advertising, an advertising network is an easy way to get started. These are companies that connect advertisers with publishers that want to display ads. Rather than you having to solicit individual companies to advertise on your site, you can sign up with an ad network that sells your site (along with the others in its network) for you. The network has the ability to sell more ads because they have more inventory to offer— your blog or site is lumped in with a group of similar sites and sold to advertisers that way. You're presented with a snippet of code to add to your site, which is how the ads are displayed. Depending on the type of advertising (CPM or CPC), you're paid based either on how many people view or click on the ads.

Google's AdSense program is a network that provides a very easy way to get started with advertising. The service will serve ads on your site; you can customize how they look and where they appear. The advertisements are drawn from Google's pool of AdWords customers—people and businesses who pay to advertise their products or services—and are designed to be relevant to the content on your site. AdSense pays you every month via electronic funds transfer or a check mailed to the address you submitted during the application process.

AdSense lets you choose the sort of ads you'd like to display on your site. You can choose between text ads or image ads, CPC ads or CPM ads. Both text and image ads can be paid on either a CPC or CPM basis. Once you've selected your ad configuration, Google will provide you with a snippet of customized JavaScript code for you to include on your site. Wherever you place this code, your ads are displayed. You'll begin earning right away.

AdSense may be the most well-known ad network, but it's not the only option for your blog or new media service. Bloggers, in particular, have a wide variety of blog-specific ad networks to choose from.

BlogAds (blogads.com) is one of the most well-known networks. However, because it has become so popular, it's now available by invitation only. You must be sponsored by a blogger who is already in the network if you want to join.

CrispAds (crispads.com) is another option. This blog-specific CPC advertising network functions similarly to AdSense: You register as a publisher, and, after installing a snippet of code, you'll display rotating text or graphic ads on your blog. CrispAds lets you select the keywords you'd like to describe your blog, and ads that target those keywords will be shown.

> **⚠ Beware!**
> Pop-ups and pop-unders are detested by the greater internet population. Even the advantage of earning revenue from every visitor can quickly be trumped by the price of annoying your readers.

▲

The ABCs (and the CPCs) of Advertising

Before you begin researching ad networks, you should be familiar with the difference between cost-per-click (CPC) advertising and cost-per-thousand (CPM) advertising. That their acronyms start with CP is the only thing that's similar about these two pricing methods.

CPC advertising networks pay you a small amount of money every time a visitor to your site clicks on one of the advertisements you display for them. This is called the conversion rate: ads clicked vs. total ads served. If, unfortunately, not one of your visitors clicks on your ads, you make no money.

The largest complaint about CPC programs is that the conversion rate, on which you depend for revenue, can hinge on factors beyond your control. If an advertisement contains errors, is unattractive or is simply written in a noncompelling manner, your revenue suffers.

The other method that ad networks use, CPM, is not based on conversion rates at all. This method is a more traditional approach to advertising revenue models in that advertisers pay website publishers a certain amount of money for every 1,000 ads displayed on their websites—whether those ads receive clicks or not. This can be a more reliable and predictable approach to collecting ad revenue because it's simply based on your site's traffic.

CPM campaigns generally aren't suited to websites that are just starting out. You'll need to establish many thousands of visitors per day before this is a lucrative option. CPC advertisements, meanwhile, work best on sites that deal in subjects concerning hot commodity items. The overwhelming majority of ad networks use one of these two methods, and both have their advantages.

Not all advertising networks are specific to blogs; many are available to any website—including new media services. Kanoodle (kanoodle.com), for example, serves text ads on a rotating basis. It uses the CrispAds method of ensuring general relevancy by asking you to select keywords that pertain to your site's subject.

AdBrite (adbrite.com) is another network for web publishers. It allows you to show text and banner ads, and includes an option to display a full-page ad to your site visitors when they view their third page on your site, but only once per day.

Other advertising networks include 24/7 Real Media (247realmedia.com), Burst Media (burstmedia.com) and Chitika (http://chitika.com). Not all advertisers offer the same services, and the amount of money you can make will vary. Do your research carefully, and make sure you select a network that fits your needs, as well as your site visitors.

Registering Users

If your service grows enough, you—or a hired salesperson—may bypass ad networks and sell your site directly to advertisers themselves. If you're planning on doing this, it will greatly benefit you to collect some information about your site's visitors.

"It's good for both users and advertisers," Marini says. "It's very important for your advertisers to be able to target ads to your audience, and it benefits your audience to see ads that are relevant."

The three key pieces of information you need about your users are their gender, age and ZIP code, Marini says. Age and gender are the two most important criteria advertisers use to target their ads, and any geographic info that allows them to deliver local ads is a plus.

To obtain this information, you'll have to get it from your site visitors. When asking your audience for personal information, Marini suggests keeping the process as quick and painless as possible. "The less you ask, the more honest they'll be," he says. All the information should be entered in a secure database; once you've collected information from a significant number of visitors, you can do a simple query to find out the average age of your users. "Based on that information, you can go to an advertiser and say 'If you're looking for teen boys, we've got a ton of them using our site,'" he says.

Marini also says that timing is key when you're trying to get users to share their personal information. "You don't want to force someone to register for your site before they even see it," he says. He suggests allowing users to browse through your site without filling out any forms. Once they go beyond that—whether they use an interactive feature, post a message or search through content, for example—you can ask them to register, he says. At that point, they've become interested enough in your service that they may be willing to provide the information you request.

You should always be upfront with users about what you plan to do with the information they provide. The best way to do this is by posting an easily accessible privacy policy on your site. Your privacy policy should include the following information:

- What information you collect
- How (or if) you plan to use that information, including what types of companies you plan to share it with
- How users can access their information, change it or have it removed
- How you protect that data

In addition, you may want to let users know if you're using cookies to collect data on site traffic and what their options are for using your service if they decline to provide you with any information.

Selling Subscriptions

If your blog or new media service is being offered as a subscription-based service, you'll also have to collect information from your users—both personal info and credit card numbers. While selling subscriptions means you'll have a continuous source of revenue, you may turn off many potential users who may be able to find similar content available elsewhere for free. If the service or blog you're providing is heavily business-oriented, you may be able to sell subscriptions to a business audience. Consumers, however, can be harder to convince.

The credit-card information you collect from your subscribers must be entered into a secure database and guarded with the utmost security. Nothing can kill a growing business more quickly than a wave of bad publicity surrounding a massive data breach.

As an alternative to making your entire blog or new media service available to subscribers only, you could try offering a partially paid service. That is, you could sell

Brand Aid

If your content lends itself to being printed on mugs, T-shirts and mouse pads, you might consider selling branded merchandise.

There are several ways to go about creating and selling your own merchandise. The first, and most obvious, is to trek down to your local T-shirt shop with a copy of your logo and that funny quip you were up all night writing, hand them over, wait a few days, and then take home 12 boxes of polyester goodies. You then take a photo of your item, price it and place it on your site. If you aren't already set up to take credit cards, you can sign up for a PayPal account or you could open an eBay Store or a Yahoo! Store.

Another option is to sign up with an on-demand branding service like CafePress.com, an online store that sells a variety of items that are basically blank canvasses for your logo, brand or funny quip. The various services available offer different items, such as mouse pads, T-shirts or bumper stickers. Each item you select to sell will be displayed with your graphics on it on the web page that the service provides you. Through this page, your readers can purchase items, which are then printed and shipped. You don't need to worry about doing anything except setting up the store and collecting the revenues. The service handles the rest.

The disadvantage of these services is that they keep a hefty percentage of the sale price. You'll end up making only $2 to $6 per item. But if you're selling hundreds of items, this isn't a bad way to pad your income. Besides, if they're saving you time by buying the blank goods, printing the items, managing sales and shipping the goods, it may be worth the cost.

membership levels that would provide exclusive content, such as different categories of content, search functions or archives. You also can try selling an ad-free version of your site.

Affiliate Programs

Affiliate programs basically function like any other form of text or banner advertising in that you're paid to place an advertisement for a service or company on your blog. They're different from most ads, though, because they require not only that your visitors click an ad, but also purchase something. You then receive a small percentage of that sale. This is a long way from simply selling advertising space in the corner of your blog.

Not all sites are suited to affiliated programs, but in some cases, they can be profitable. Say you write a blog that discusses the latest bestselling mystery novels and your recommendations pull some weight with your readers. Devoting a portion of your blog site's real estate to an ad that shows recently reviewed books with an Amazon.com Associates affiliate "Buy

⚠ Beware!
Affiliate programs with unknown companies may not be lucrative. Search for programs with large retailers like Amazon and eBay.

It Now" link may do very well for you. You would need a lot of visitors and a lot of sales for the percentage you earn per sale to add up, but if you can beef up those two factors, this is a viable option.

As you can see, even your free new media service or blog has several possibilities for making a profit. Making money isn't easy, no matter how you go about it, but with a little hard work, you'll find it very possible.

Financial
Sense

Money, of course, is fun. Making it is fun. Spending it is fun. Managing it, however, is not always a good time. When you're running a business, though, careful money management is an absolute necessity.

Managing Your Finances

You may be very organized when it comes to keeping track of your personal finances. Maybe you're already using a personal finance application, tracking your income and expenses according to meticulously mapped-out categories. Or maybe you've got a checkbook—somewhere, you're not sure exactly where you last saw it—and a wallet full of creased, torn and tattered receipts. Whatever works for keeping track of your personal finances is fine, but the same can't be said when it comes to your business. You absolutely must keep detailed records of any and all financial transactions.

To learn about the basics of bookkeeping, please read the "Keeping Score" chapter in *Startup Basics*. This will provide you with all the background information you need to manage your company's books. It provides information on the two most common accounting methods: cash-based accounting and accrual-based accounting. Let's talk about these methods in a bit more detail, though, as they relate to your net service.

As the owner of a service-based business, you don't have to worry about inventory. This makes your life much simpler when it comes to keeping your books; it's one less thing to track. It also gives you the option of choosing between these two basic accounting methods. If your business carries an inventory (or if you're structured as a corporation or exceed $5 million in annual sales), you must use the accrual-based method.

The advantage of the cash-based method of accounting is that it's simpler: You track expenses when they occur and income when it's received. This method makes sense for many sole proprietors. However, it can provide a skewed picture of your business's financial state, especially when you're providing services. That's because you may provide your service to clients in August but not receive the payment for it until November. So your financial statements for August may show you operating at a loss. Similarly, your financial statements for November could be falsely positive if you're receiving payments for older accounts but not actually selling any new services.

That's why many service-based businesses opt for the accrual method. Income is reported when the service is offered, not when it's actually paid for. This method provides a more accurate picture of your business's financial state. For example, if you design websites for four clients in April, but only one client in June, your financial statements will accurately reflect April as a more positive month, no matter when those clients actually pay their bills.

Accounting and bookkeeping can bewilder even the savviest entrepreneurs. Whenever you need help, ask a professional. Don't hesitate.

Smart Tip

Tip...

Using the accrual-based method of accounting helps you focus on how well you're selling your service, rather than simply on how much money you're taking in.

Operating Expenses

How much it costs you to run your net service can vary greatly. We already told you that you can start a blog for as little as, well, nothing, but we also told you that you might need $500,000 on hand to start a new media service. What accounts for the drastic difference in expenses? Here's a breakdown of where that money will go.

Website Design

In Chapter 2 of this book, we told you that you'll need to spend about $5,200 to start a full-time, homebased web design company. That total assumes you need to purchase everything—including the necessary computer and hardware to run your business—so the good news for many entrepreneurs is that starting this business can be done relatively cheaply. What's even better is that for the first few years, running your company likely won't cost you much more than your initial investment.

As a freelance website designer, insurance may be one of your most significant expenses—if you need to purchase you own health insurance, that is. Purchasing health insurance for you or your family can be prohibitively expensive when you don't have an employer sharing the costs with you. If you're planning to leave your current job where you do have insurance coverage, you may be able to use COBRA, a federal program designed to ensure insurance coverage for up to 18 months post-employment. COBRA isn't cheap, however; you'll be paying what your employer paid, so it can cost you anywhere from a few hundred to more than a thousand dollars per month.

Purchasing health insurance directly from a private company is likely to be very costly, too, so using an organization designed for freelancers or the self-employed may be a better option; you can find plans that run anywhere from $200 to $700 per month for individuals.

You'll also need to spend some money on liability insurance for your business—luckily, this is significantly less expensive than health insurance. A policy will cost you anywhere from $500 to about $1,500 per year. Your solo web design shop likely won't need any additional insurance coverage, but you should check the limits and restrictions on your homeowners insurance if you're operating your business out of your home. Your policy may cover business equipment stored in your home

> **Bright Idea**
>
> If you need health insurance, look for an organization like Freelancers Union (freelancersunion.org) or eHealthInsurance (ehealthinsurance.com) that helps freelancers and independent contractors purchase coverage at lower rates than private companies offer.

office, but it may not—especially if your home office is located in a building that's separate from the main structure of your house, such as a garage.

Website Design Service Expenses

Item	Annual Cost
Office space	$0
Computer hardware	$1,700*
Computer software	$2,000*
Office supplies/equipment	$700*
Internet access	$540
Phone service	$540
Domain name registration	$9*
Website hosting	$84
Advertising	$500
Health insurance	$3,600
Business insurance	$1,000
Subtotal	$6,264
Miscellaneous expenses (10 percent of subtotal)	$626
Total	**$6,890**

*One-time fees, usually incurred at startup

Your next significant expense will be paying for a dedicated office phone line and high-speed internet access. Both those services will run you about $45 per month each, so you can expect to spend about $540 per year on each of them. You can also expect to spend about $7 per month ($84 per year) on web hosting fees.

Other fees you may encounter include the cost of hiring an attorney to review any sample contracts and legal forms you may have; you can expect to spend about $200 for a very basic review. It's unlikely that you'll require the services of an accountant when your business is this small.

Despite the small size of your business— or perhaps because of it—you may want to invest in some advertising. Using classified

Dollar Stretcher

Already have automobile or homeowner's insurance? Ask your agent if they also offer insurance plans for your business. You may be able to get a discount for purchasing another policy.

Quick! Quicken or QuickBooks?

Quicken and QuickBooks. The names sure sound alike. Both applications come from Intuit. Does that mean they do the same thing? Hardly. Quicken and QuickBooks are two very different tools, but both can be very handy for small-business owners.

Quicken (http://quicken.intuit.com) is primarily a personal finance manager, but it also comes in a Home & Business version that can be used by sole proprietors. It allows you to see both your personal and business finances in one view, which can be handy if these finances are closely related—if you're running a very small blogging business, for example. Quicken also includes limited invoicing capabilities.

QuickBooks (http://quickbooks.intuit.com) is a far more robust business accounting package. It uses the double-entry accounting system preferred by many business owners. This system records each transaction in two accounts, once as a credit and once as a debit. (You can use QuickBooks as a single-entry accounting system if your needs are simpler.) It also allows you to generate more extensive financial reports, offers a complete inventory and payroll system, and supports multiple users.

Your choice in accounting software isn't limited to these two applications, however. Keep in mind that many other excellent accounting applications are available. Sage Software offers the Peachtree (peachtree.com) line of accounting applications, including a version targeted at very small businesses just switching over from a manual accounting system. Microsoft offers Office Accounting (microsoft.com), MYOB offers Premier Accounting (myob-us.com), and NetSuite (netsuite.com) offers a complete hosted accounting and business management system.

sites like Craigslist is free; advertising in newspapers can run you anywhere from as little as $50 to several thousand dollars. Using online advertising services like Google AdWords, you can spend anywhere from $50 to $5,000 per month. A reasonable advertising budget for this business would be about $500 to $1,000 per year.

As you can see, running a small web design shop isn't prohibitively expensive. Check out the chart above that lists the expenses you can expect in your first year, including your startup costs.

▲

A Penny Saved

As an entrepreneur, you should always be looking for ways to cut costs. Here are a few things you can do to save money while running your business—especially in the early days.

- Wait as long as you can before you lease office space.
- If you need office space, consider a sublease. Look for a company that may have taken on more space than it needs right now and see if you can make arrangements to sublease part of their office. This will save you money, help you avoid signing a long-term lease, and offer the added bonus of allowing you and your staff to be around like-minded entrepreneurs.
- If your business doesn't require a lot of contact with the outside world in its very early stages, skip paying for pricey phone service. Rely on your cell phone and have employees do the same; you can reimburse them if necessary.
- Substitute free software for paid applications. Skip Microsoft Office; opt for OpenOffice (openoffice.org) or Google Docs (http://documents.google.com) instead. Don't buy an Exchange server for e-mail; instead, use Google Mail (gmail.com).

Search Engine Marketing

The operating expenses for your SEM company will depend largely on the structure you choose. If you decide to operate a solo consultancy, many of your expenses will be similar to the costs of running a solo web design shop, as detailed in the previous section. Should you set up an agency with a few employees, however, your costs will be quite different. And, yes, different means higher.

One of the biggest expenses will be leasing office space. If your firm will be small (less than five employees), leasing office space probably won't be prohibitively expensive. According to most estimates, you need about 200 to 250 square feet of office space for each employee. That means you'll want to find an office that's between 1,000 and 1,250 square feet.

Office space is typically priced per square foot (on an annual basis), and those prices will vary depending on the location and class of the space in question. (See "Making The Grade" in Chapter 9 for more information on the different classes of office space.) The average cost of all office space in Detroit,

Dollar Stretcher

Locating your office in the suburbs can help you save on office rent.

for example, is $19.50 per square foot. Class A office space in Detroit averages $24 per square foot. In comparison, the average cost of office space in San Francisco is $35.90 per square foot, and Class A office space can range from $40 per square foot to upward of $80 per square foot.

For our calculations, we'll estimate that you're going to pay $25 per square foot, and we'll assume that your rent includes all the furniture you'll need, plus any utilities and building fees. At that rate, a 1,000 square foot office will cost you about $2,083 per month. You can adjust that figure up or down depending on where your business is located and what type of office space you're looking for.

Another significant expense will be your employees. For this example, we'll say you have three employees and are paying each of them $40,000 per year. Don't assume you can budget $120,000 in employee compensation costs, however. You also have to factor in their benefits and the taxes you'll have to pay on them. You can figure about $5,000 to $10,000 per employee for this. That means your total cost for three employees with salaries of $40,000 per year will be about $140,000.

Additionally, you'll need to pay for

Smart Tip

Traveling to industry events and conferences can be expensive. But getting your name out there and networking with other professionals is an investment in your company's future.

general liability insurance, as well as Errors & Omissions coverage. Annual premiums for this type of coverage can run anywhere from $3,000 to $10,000. We'll put $6,000 on our budget.

As we mentioned in Chapter 3, you'll need to spend about $1,000 to $1,500 per employee on computers at startup. Software will cost you about $1,000 to $2,000 upfront, and you can estimate another $400 to $500 per month for the subscription-based SEO and SEM tools you'll need. Add about $2,000 for two servers for your office and $500 for any printers, copiers and fax machines, and your total spending on all this technology in your first year will come to about $13,000. That's a significant investment.

Your monthly expenses will also include the cost of phone service for your office (about $200 to $500 per month) and internet access (a business-class DSL package costs about $150 per month). You can budget about $3,600 per year for phone service and $1,800 per year for internet access. Registering your domain name will cost you about $9; we'll assume you're going to host your own website on one of your servers, so we won't add in any hosting fees.

SEM Agency Expenses

Item	Annual Cost
Office space	$25,000
Employees	$140,000*
Business insurance	$6,000
Internet access	$3,600
Phone service	$1,800
Travel	$6,000
Advertising	$2,000
Computer hardware	$6,500*
Computer software	$6,800*
Legal fees	$750*
Accounting fees	$3,000*
Office supplies/equipment	$1,500*
Domain name registration	$9*
Subtotal	$184,400
Miscellaneous expenses (10 percent of subtotal)	$18,440
Total	**$202,840**

*One-time fees, usually incurred at startup

You'll likely need to travel to visit clients and to attend industry events and conferences. A healthy travel budget would be about $500 per month or $6,000 per year. Advertising costs will be less than that; you can use those conferences and events to network and sell your services. You may also want to do some dedicated advertising of your own, both online and elsewhere. Estimate about $1,000 to $2,000 for an annual advertising budget.

You should budget about $750 to $1,000 to have an attorney review your business agreement, incorporate your business (or set up your partnership), and review the contracts you plan to use with your clients. You'll also likely need an accountant to help set up your books and review your business plan. Accountants charge anywhere from $50 to $400 an hour. You can estimate that it will take about 10 to 20 hours to get your financial system up and running, and 15 to 30 hours to review your business plan and work on its financial statements. If you pay $150 an hour, that's about $2,250 for setting up your books and $3,000 for your business plan.

As you can see in the following chart, running an SEM agency with four to five employees will cost you just over $200,000 per year.

New Media Service

Running a new media startup has the potential to bring in great financial rewards. It also has the potential to empty your wallet. Operating this kind of company isn't cheap. Here's a look at where that money will go.

Employee salaries are your biggest expense. We'll say you've hired five people and plan to pay them $60,000 per year. Add in the taxes and benefits, and you can estimate a cost of about $75,000 per employee. That's a total of $375,000 annually.

Office space will also be costly. You'll need about 1,500 square feet; if you pay $35 per square foot, your monthly rent will be about $4,375. We'll round that up to $5,000 per month to account for any utilities, common fees and furniture charges you may need to pay.

Dollar Stretcher

Look for a sublease on office space. It can save you money and prevent you from getting locked into a long-term contract.

Other ongoing expenses include about $500 to $600 per month for internet access (using a dedicated T1 line); anywhere from $500 to $2,000 per month for phone service; and annual premiums of $7,000 to $10,000 for liability and E&O insurance.

Your upfront costs, which we explained in Chapter 4, include purchasing the necessary hardware and software to run your new media service. Outfitting your staff with desktops or laptops will run you about $7,000 to $10,000; you can expect to spend another $5,000 to $10,000 on servers. Depending on your needs, software can also be pricey; a database application alone can run several thousand dollars. Estimate anywhere from $5,000 to $15,000 for software. Add in about $500 to $1,000 for any printers, copiers or fax machines you may need.

Additional upfront expenses include office supplies and equipment ($2,000 to $5,000) and the cost to register your domain name (a bargain at $9). You'll also pay about $1,000 to $1,500 to have an attorney review your business structure and incorporate your company or create your partnership (this includes the fees for registering with your state government). Should you plan on offering stock options to your employees or otherwise selling ownership stake in your company, you should have an attorney either create or review those documents. That can cost $1,000 or more, depending on the complexity of the arrangements.

If you're seeking VC funding, you'll need an accountant to review your business plan and draft your financial statements. This can take anywhere from 20 to 60 hours,

New Media Service Expenses

Item	Annual Cost
Office rent and utilties	$60,000
Desktop/laptop computers	$7,000*
Servers and printers	$7,500*
Computer software	$10,000*
Office supplies/equipment	$4,000*
Internet access	$6,000
Phone service	$6,000
Business insurance	$7,000
Legal fees	$2,500*
Accounting fees	$15,000
Domain name registration	$9*
Employee salaries	$375,000
Subtotal	$469,000
Miscellaneous expenses (10 percent of subtotal)	$46,900
Total	**$515,900**

*One-time fees, usually incurred at startup

depending on the complexity of your organization. At $150 per hour, you can expect to spend about $6,000. You also may need to meet with your accountant on a regular basis—say quarterly—to make sure that your finances are on track as you seek funding or apply the funds you receive. Estimate about 15 hours each quarter; at $150 an hour, that comes out to $9,000 for the year.

Suddenly, $500,000 doesn't seem like an exorbitant budget! See the breakdown for where it all will go.

Blogging Business

In Chapter 5, we told you that you can expect to spend less than $700 to start a small blogging business (and that's if you need to buy a computer), and about $2,000 to start a bigger blogging business. Starting a blog is cheap, and so, too, is running it.

Beware!
Don't go without health insurance, even if you're young and healthy. It's just too risky.

After your initial startup expenses for your basic blog (which include purchasing a simple computer and some minor office supplies), your operating expenses will be only about $540 per year: That's the price you can expect to pay for a high-speed internet connection.

If your blogging ambitions are bigger, running your business will be slightly more expensive. We estimated that you'll spend just about $2,000 getting your company up and running. That includes purchasing a very good desktop computer; outfitting your home office with furniture, equipment and all the necessary supplies; and registering your domain name.

Blogging Business Expenses

Item	Annual Cost
Office rent and utilties	$0
Desktop/laptop computers	$1,000*
Software	$90
Office supplies/equipment	$700*
Internet access	$540
Phone service	$540
Copyright registration fee	$35*
Domain name registration	$9*
Website hosting	$84
Hosted blogging application	$90
Health insurance	$3,600
Liability insurance	$2,500
Contributors	$1,200
Subtotal	$8,464
Miscellaneous expenses (10 percent of subtotal)	$864
Total	**$9,310**

*One-time fees, usually incurred at startup

Your monthly expenses will include $45 per month each for internet access an phone service, as well as $7 per month for website hosting. You should also budget about $9 to $20 per month for a hosted blogging application that allows you to map a URL to your own domain name. TypePad's Plus account offers that feature, and costs $89.50 for one year.

If you'll need to purchase health insurance, plan to spend about $300 per month (at least) on that. Your blogging business itself may not need any insurance coverage. Depending on your content, however, you may want to consider media liability insurance. This type of policy covers the costs of lawsuits brought against you for defamation, copyright infringement and more. An annual premium may run $2,500 per year, and some insurance companies will require you to hire a lawyer to analyze your risk of being sued before they'ill provide coverage.

As your business grows, you'll likely start paying contributors to post content. You can expect to pay them between $5 and $15 per post in most cases.

As you can see in the chart on page 145, running a blog can be done without spending very much money at all. Now that's a nice change.

Sales Tax Talk

You may think that you don't need to worry about sales tax because you're operating an internet-based, service-oriented business. Think again. In some cases, you absolutely may be responsible for collecting sales tax from your customers and paying that to various states. But calling sales tax laws confusing would be putting it mildly; the laws vary—and vary drastically—from state to state.

"There's a lot of conflicting information out there, both on the web and in the media," says Diane Yetter, the owner of Chicago-based Yetter Consulting Services, a company that helps businesses understand their sales tax obligations. "It's not surprising that many people don't understand the rules."

Not understanding the rules can land

> **Tip...**
>
> **Smart Tip**
> Sales tax laws are confusing. Enlisting the help of a professional can save you time—and in the long run, it may save you money, too.

you—and your company—in hot water. "Never assume that sales tax doesn't apply to you," Yetter advises. "If you don't collect the tax from your customers, the states can hold you responsible for it, plus interest and penalties. That could be enough to put a small business out of business."

So your first order of business when it comes to sales tax is navigating the often murky laws of the various states to figure out in which states you have a sales tax responsibility. There are two key factors that will make you responsible for collecting and paying sales tax, Yetter says. The first is whether you have nexus in a state. The second is whether the service you're offering is taxable.

Nexus means that your business has some sort of physical connection to a state or a minimum level of activity in that state, which generally means you must have some sort of physical presence before you can be held responsible for collecting and paying sales tax. But different types of a physical presence can constitute nexus in different states, and as the operator of a virtual business, you need to consider this carefully.

"If you're talking about a service-based business, what constitutes a physical presence can vary so much," Yetter says. "If you travel and visit customers, you're creating a physical presence wherever you go. But states vary on how much presence constitutes nexus. In Texas, for example, all you have to do is step foot in the state to establish nexus. If you go there for one day to attend a trade show, you've established nexus. If you go to California for two days and attend a trade show, it's not likely that you've established nexus. However, if you go to California and perform services and meet with your clients for three days, it's very likely that California will say you have nexus."

What it comes down to is this: "It depends on the activity, and the state in which you're conducting that activity," Yetter says.

Should you have remote workers in any state, your business will have nexus there, Yetter notes. Even if they work out of their homes and are not in any way related to the sale of your service, an employee still constitutes nexus, she says.

Figuring out if you have nexus is only the first step toward determining if you need to collect sales tax; now you need to figure out if your service is taxable in any of the states where you do have nexus. Again, this varies drastically.

Anything that's sold by a company can be divided into three categories, Yetter says: tangible goods, intangible goods, and services. Tangible goods, which are typically products that you'd ship to your customers, are generally taxable, with various exceptions. Your net service likely won't be delivering tangible goods, so we don't need to discuss this in detail.

You may be delivering intangible goods, however, and you definitely will be delivering a service, so let's explain the difference between these two categories. Intangible goods, according to Yetter, are typically items that would be downloaded over the internet, like electronic books, software or digital music. Some states tax intangible goods; some do not. Services are not actual products; a service is work that you perform for someone else. In most cases, your service will be performed remotely. Again, some states tax services while others do not.

You must clearly research the laws of any state in which you have nexus to find out if your service is taxable and at what

> **Beware!**
> You should never collect sales tax if you're not legally registered to do so in that state. This is considered criminal fraud.

rate it's taxed. You're responsible for collecting the right amount of tax from your clients and holding it until it's time to turn it over to the state. You must also find out whether you're delivering any intangible goods; in some cases, the software updates or information you provide to your clients could fall into that category.

And remember that just because your home state may not consider your service taxable, you're not free from any burden. Yetter offers this example: Illinois doesn't consider a website design service taxable. So if you're a developer in Illinois, any work you perform for clients in Illinois isn't taxable, so you don't need to worry about Illinois sales tax.

South Dakota, however, considers website design a taxable service. If a client in South Dakota wants to hire you, you may be responsible for collecting sales tax but only if you have nexus in that state. If you go to South Dakota for a week to meet with your client and learn about their business, you've established nexus—even if you do all the actual web design work back in Illinois. You're now responsible for collecting sales tax in South Dakota.

If you've never stepped foot in South Dakota, have no employees there, and definitely haven't established nexus there, you don't need to worry about collecting sales tax. Your client in South Dakota is responsible for paying use tax on your service, however.

A use tax is a tax levied by a state that's designed to compensate for sales tax lost when an item is purchased outside of a state but used within that state, according to legal website Nolo.com. If you don't have nexus in a state, your clients bear the burden of use tax. This is entirely their responsibility. Keep in mind, however, that this means your service is not really "tax free" and shouldn't be advertised as such; it's just that the burden of paying the tax has been shifted to your customers. You're not responsible for reminding them to pay it. Most companies, especially bigger ones, are aware of these laws and will pay the necessary use taxes, Yetter says. But you do a disservice if you falsely advertise your internet-based service as tax free.

Collecting and Paying Taxes

The process of collecting sales tax and paying it to each state to which you're responsible can be a relatively painless process, though it, too, varies by state. The first thing you need to do is to register with each state where you've established nexus. You can find information on how to register at the Department of Revenue website for each state. In some states, you can complete the entire process online, while other states will require you to mail in certain forms, Yetter says. She also notes that some states have a very brief form for you to fill out, while others have longer forms; Pennsylvania, she notes, has a form that's more than 20 pages long.

In general, you'll need to provide your federal employer ID number, as well as some basic information about your business, including an estimate of your taxable sales. You may also be asked for the names of officers in your company, which parties will be responsible for the sales tax, and what types of activities you'll be conducting in the state.

If you register with a state, they'll assume you want to be registered, Yetter notes. A state isn't likely to come back to you and tell you that your activity doesn't constitute nexus and you're not responsible for collecting sales tax. Some companies may register with a state where they don't have nexus in order to collect sales tax for a customer who knows they'll need to pay the use tax. Having the company register and collect the tax up front makes it easier for these customers (usually businesses) to pay their taxes, so the companies do it voluntarily. So do your homework before registering and make sure you're really responsible for collecting sales tax in that state.

Once you're registered, the state will set you up on a "filing frequency," Yetter says. This refers to how often you'll be responsible for paying the sales tax you've collected from your clients. Small companies may pay sales tax monthly, quarterly, semi-annually or even annually, Yetter notes. The process of filing is simpler than filing a tax return in most states, she says.

As you can see, the laws surrounding sales tax are difficult to navigate and can be a challenge even for experts. There's no central source that provides information on all the tax laws of each state; your best bet is to visit the website for the Department of Revenue in each state you're concerned about, Yetter says. You can also turn to your lawyer and your accountant for advice.

Hiring
Employees

M any of you may be starting your net service with no intention of ever hiring employees, and that's a perfectly viable option. But if you would like to grow your business beyond the limits of a one-person company, here's what you need to know.

Building a Staff

Earlier in this book, in each of the chapters specific to the types of net service you might start, we discussed when you might need to hire employees. Essentially, when it's time to hire, you'll know it. There will come a point when you know you need help—either to sell your service, to manage your database, or to build a website that brings your plan for a new media service to life. Whatever the reason, you'll know when the time has arrived to make your first hire.

Whom to Hire

When the time arrives, how will you know whom to hire? You'll want people who provide the skills and have the experience necessary to fulfill the job functions. Beyond that, however, you need to keep in mind that you're hiring people you'll likely be spending a whole lot of time with. So you need to make sure that your personalities and work ethics gel.

"Keeping the jerks out is a big deal," says Tickle.com's Rick Marini. "People need to be smart, hard working, fun. They need to have integrity and share my passion. If I find those qualities, I feel good. I have to find people I want to be around 80 hours a week. So I don't want people who are going to kill the culture."

Also important, Marini says, is finding people who have the drive to work for a startup. "The people I'm recruiting all want to be entrepreneurs. They want to come in on the ground floor and have the ability to shape the company every day," he says.

Depending on the type of net service you're launching—and where you're located—you may have trouble finding people to hire. UpWord SEM's Robert Cavilla says that experienced SEO staff can be very hard to find. Many experienced search engine marketers will find they can make more money freelancing, so they're reluctant to work in-house anywhere. Another problem is that many of the big players in this area will make their employees sign noncompete agreements, so even if these employees are willing to come work for your firm, they may not legally be allowed to do so for a specified period of time after leaving their existing job.

One way around this is to hire intelligent people and train them, Cavilla notes. "We've hired people who may have a limited amount of search marketing experience, but they have good marketing experience or good overall professional experience, and we train them," he says. "We try to hire the smartest people we can find."

How to Hire

The first thing you need to do when planning to hire an employee is sit down and specify exactly what role you're looking to fill. Write a job description with as much detail as you can. Determine what the employee's duties will be; from there, you can figure out what skills and experience they'll need to fill the role. Try to figure out what skills they can learn on the job and which ones they'll need to bring with them. Remember: How much time and patience you have to help them learn will go a long way in determining this.

You also need to figure out the pay. You need to determine what salary or hourly rate you can offer, based both on what you can afford and what the industry offers. You also need to decide what kind of schedule you'll expect the employee to work.

Next, you should advertise the job opening. You can use traditional methods, like newspaper ads and job websites, to find candidates, but be prepared for a flood of responses—often from less-than-qualified candidates. You can also advertise in industry-specific publications and websites. You should use your industry network to find qualified candidates, too. Talk to friends and colleagues, and let them know you're hiring. They may be able to refer someone.

When scheduling interviews, you'll want to make sure you're interviewing enough candidates so you have several contenders to choose from but not so many that you become overwhelmed and unable to remember whom you've interviewed. If you already have other employees, ask them to meet with potential candidates, too, so you have more than one opinion on which to base your decision.

Following an interview, you should check references and a candidate's employment history to verify the informa-

Bright Idea

If you're overwhelmed with responses to your job ad, try scheduling phone interviews. This can help you screen out candidates who aren't a good fit for you more quickly. A phone interview shouldn't take the place of a face-to-face interview when hiring, though—it's just the first step.

tion they provided. Taking the time to do this now could save you many hassles down the road. You should also schedule a second interview with potential hires. Meeting someone for an hour isn't always enough time to determine whether or not they're someone you can work with for the foreseeable future.

Once you've decided to hire someone, you can extend an offer informally, over the phone, to see if it'll be accepted. Be prepared for some negotiations, whether over salary, benefits or a starting date. Once the offer has been accepted, you should formalize it in a written agreement for your records.

▲

When a job interview is going well, you may find that the conversation becomes informal. This may seem like a great sign that the candidate is a good fit. Unfortunately, it also means you run the risk of asking a question that's illegal in the context of a job interview. Even the most casual question—like "Where are you from?"—can violate discrimination laws.

Remember, it's illegal to ask any questions during a job interview that may be considered discriminatory, specifically those related to a candidate's birthplace, age, race, gender, religion, marital status or disability. If you're unfamiliar with the laws surrounding job interviews, do your homework before you begin the hiring process. Even if you are familiar with these laws, you may forget about them if an interview veers into informal territory. This is a good reason to keep the chit-chat to a minimum during job interviews.

What Types of Employees Should You Hire?

Now that we've given you a brief overview of how to hire employees, let's talk about the types of employees you may need. Not everyone will start out by hiring full-time, permanent help right away. In some cases, it may make more sense to hire a temporary worker or an independent contractor who works for you on a project basis.

Permanent employees: Permanent employees can be hired on a part-time or full-time basis, and can be paid hourly wages or a salary. If you hire a permanent employee, you're responsible for complying with federal, state and perhaps even city laws regarding withholding income taxes, withholding and paying Social Security and Medicare taxes, and paying unemployment taxes on the wages you pay. Wages for permanent employees must be reported on a W-2 form.

Some business owners think they can save money by hiring temporary workers or using independent contractors. While this may be true in some cases, hiring permanent employees can make more sense in many situations. If a project is going to last longer than a few months, you may be better off hiring a permanent employee. You have more control over their work, you don't need to worry about training new workers constantly, and you have the chance to build and nurture a relationship with the employee. A positive relationship between employer and employee benefits everyone.

Temporary employees: Temporary workers, or "temps," can be hired directly or through an agency. They're brought on to help for a set amount of time, whether on a specific project or to get your business through a busy period.

The most common—and, often, the easiest—way to hire temps is through an agency. You pay a premium for this arrangement, but it does have its benefits. You hire the agency, and they handle the rest. They screen and hire workers and take care of payroll taxes and employee benefits. Hiring temps gives you the flexibility to add help quickly when needed. You may also be able to hire temporary employees to work for you on a perma-

> **Tip...**
>
> **Smart Tip**
>
> If your job is expected to last six months or longer, you'll likely save money by hiring a permanent employee rather than a temp.

nent basis after you've evaluated their skills, but doing so may require negotiating with and paying a fee to the agency that supplied the worker.

Independent contractors: Independent contractors, like temporary workers, allow you to quickly add staff to your business. An independent contractor is an individual (or in some cases, another business) who provides services for your company but is not an employee. Hiring an independent contractor has some financial benefits for you, as you're not responsible for withholding or paying any taxes on payments you make to them. For that reason, the IRS has very strict laws governing who can—and can't—be considered an independent contractor.

So who can be considered an independent contractor? According to the IRS, "A general rule is that you, the payer, have the right to control or direct only the result of the work done by an independent contractor and not the means or methods of accomplishing the result."

In contrast, the IRS uses the following definition for an employee: "A general rule is that anyone who performs services for you is your employee if you can control what will be done and how it will be done."

Supervision of and control over the work that's done is one factor used to determine whether or not that worker is an independent contractor, but other factors are also considered. The amount of skill required to do the work, the length of the contract, the location of the worker, and whether or not the employer provides the tools, instruments and equipment necessary to complete the work are all taken into account when making the determination.

Hiring an independent contractor can make sense for your business—if you do it right. You can quickly get help to complete your projects without going through the trouble of finding, hiring and providing benefits for a full-time employee. Hiring contractors may also be one of the best, if not the only, way to find the experienced help you need in certain situations. UpWord's Cavilla notes that his SEM firm had to rely on contract help because many experienced search engine marketers were reluctant to accept in-house positions anywhere. They had become accustomed to working their own hours from their own locations, and found that they could make more money doing this than by accepting offers for full-time employment.

But you should always use caution when hiring contractors, especially if you plan to do so for an extended period of time. The IRS warns: "If you incorrectly classify an employee as an independent contractor, you can be held liable for employment taxes for that worker, plus a penalty."

Payments in excess of $600 made to an independent contractor are reported on Form 1099-MISC, Miscellaneous Income. Before reporting payments on the 1099 form, you should have contractors fill out form W-9; this allows you to get their taxpayer identification number (usually their Social Security number). You can download Form W-9 from the IRS' website at irs.gov.

Interns: Depending on the location of your business and the type of work you need done, hiring an intern could be a possibility. Generally, an intern is an undergraduate or graduate student looking to gain experience in a certain field. When you hire an intern, you typically do so for a set period of time—a semester or the summer, for example. Many interns work for course credit alone, so you may not have to pay them.

Aside from the budgetary bonus, hiring an intern can have other benefits. You may find that an intern has a fresh, enthusiastic take on the working world. They haven't been disillusioned by years of working. On the flip side, however, you may find that your intern needs more guidance and direction than the average employee. You may also want to spend a bit more time providing this help to your interns; remember that while you're relying on them for help with your business, they're also looking at the internship as a way to gain skills and experience in the workplace.

You can talk to the employment or career development offices at local colleges and universities if you're thinking about hiring an intern. When considering candidates and conducting interviews, you should use many of the same criteria as if you were hiring a permanent employee. While an intern may not have the skills and experience yet, you should look for a candidate who is smart enough to learn on the job, and for someone with a personality and mindset that will fit in your office environment.

Contributors: Bloggers are likely to feel a great pressure to produce a steady stream of content. That's where contributors come in. You can either pay contributors a per-posting fee (typically $5 on up) or ask for volunteers.

One of the best places to find volunteer contributors is among your readership. The people who visit your blog regularly have already displayed a sincere interest in your content. There are probably a few among them who would love a chance to begin writing for their favorite blog. There's a thrill in being a reader-turned-poster; most readers would jump at the chance to post to the blog without pay. This may seem like a wonderful situation, and it may well be, but you should be careful when accepting volunteer help.

First, you'll have a hard time imposing quotas on volunteer help. Asking for daily content from volunteers may be asking too much. And, if you decide that the volunteer you've enlisted isn't producing the quality of post you would like, you'll have a harder time asking him to stop. Paying contributors, even a small stipend, makes it easier to set a minimum number of posts per day and to "fire" writers who don't produce quality posts.

Stat Fact

Job creation in Professional and Business Services and Information Technology is expected to increase in coming years. According to a recent survey by CareerBuilder. com, 45 percent of employers in this area plan to add jobs in the coming years.

You should plan to serve as editor for any bloggers you hire, at least for a short period of time, to evaluate the quality of the content they'll produce for you. You cannot take the risk of hiring help without editorial rights. Your blog could suffer heavily from an incompetent, unreliable or uninformed blogger. Until you can trust that a certain person will reliably produce worthy content for you, insist that everything he or she posts passes through you first. This will create more work for you in the short term, as you'll be writing your own posts while editing others, but it will pay off in the long run if you can find reliable help.

If you're able to find several reliable contributors—enough to cover your daily posting duties—you could conceivably get out of posting to your blog altogether and focus on finding more readers, advertisers and, therefore, profits. That is, if that's the part of the blogging business you like best.

A Virtual Office

If you hire independent contractors for your net service, they likely won't be working out of your office. Did you know that the same can be true of your permanent employees, though? Your business is virtual, so maybe you should think about creating a virtual office, too.

Hiring And Supervising Remote Employees

A remote employee is one who doesn't work out of your company's main office. If you don't have office space, then all your employees may be remote—in fact, using remote employees is one way to save on office space altogether. More commonly, though, most of your employees will be based out of a central location, with a few remote employees who work elsewhere, whether from their home or another office.

Why hire remote workers? Because you want to hire the best person for the job, not simply the best person in your area. If your SEM company is based in Texas but you find a skilled practitioner who lives in Connecticut, you may think your only option is to convince him to move to Texas. It's not: Let him work from his home. Treat him as you would any other permanent employee, albeit one you must communicate with via e-mail and phone, rather than face-to-face.

When hiring a remote employee, you may want to meet him in person before offering him the job. This isn't necessary, but it can help both parties feel more comfortable with the arrangement. His salary and benefits should be dealt with as if he were working out of your office; so, too, should her job expectations.

Be up front about what you expect from your remote workers: If they're in a different time zone, let them know if you want them available during your business hours or if they're free to work on their own schedules. You should also let them know how much communication you expect from them and what kinds of status reports or updates you require on a regular basis.

Remember that you need to be able to trust all your employees, especially your remote workers. If a virtual office arrangement is going to work out for you, you must have faith that your employees are doing what you ask of them—no matter where they are. A remote employee may not be coming into the office every day, but that doesn't mean they aren't getting the job done. Remember, it's just as easy for an office worker to be slacking off, right under your nose.

> **Dollar Stretcher**
>
> When working with remote employees, use one of the many free instant messaging programs available to keep in touch. This is a convenient— and cheap—way to maintain communication.

Working with a Remote Team

When you're working with remote employees, you should keep in mind that they need to feel like a real part of your team. Do your best to make them feel involved. Invest in a good speaker phone that will allow them to really take part in team meetings and other conferences. You should also consider having them visit your office from time to time. Even an occasional face-to-face meeting goes a long way toward building a good professional relationship.

Beyond the professional aspects of the job, however, you'll want to make sure your remote workers feel involved with and connected to their co-workers. Encourage everyone to use the phone rather than e-mail when it makes sense, and keep everyone up-to-date on what's new in the office.

How to Compete with Employee Benefits

You may think that finding the right employees for your net service was the hard part. Think again: Now you have to keep them around. And that can be harder than you think. For information on offering health insurance and creating a retirement plan for your employees, read the "Perk Up" chapter in *Startup Basics*.

Health insurance is a key benefit to be sure, but many net services will be staffed by younger employees with other priorities. They also may not see the benefit of staying in one place for a long time. These workers may also feel the lure of bigger companies—like Google—that can hire whomever they want, pay them a whole lot, and offer plenty of perks you may not be able to afford.

"Google is an awesome place to work," says Tickle's Rick Marini. "We lost people to them, but we've also pulled people out."

What can you do to compete? See what works for those companies, and try to incorporate what you can into your own company. You may not be able to offer an on-site doctor, gym or dry cleaner like Google does, but just as important as these perks is the fact that Google is known for offering an employee-friendly environment: "They care about their employees. They treat them like valued employees," Marini says. He tries to do the same at his business. "It's a great way to attract people," says Marini. "If you value your employees, the people who work at your company will convey that to others."

Beyond treating employees with respect and dignity, Marini also offers more concrete benefits. "You have to give people the chance to have an impact. As an entrepreneur, you walk a fine line. You have your ideas and you stick to them, but you also need to allow the people you've hired to have input. The best way to build a company quickly is to hire the right people and let them succeed. Don't micromanage," he says.

> **Fun Fact**
> Google offers its employees free meals in its cafeteria, and its main office offers an on-site oil change and car wash, as well as a dry cleaner and a hairstylist.

A very concrete way to allow your employees to feel the results of their hard work is to offer stock options. This allows employees to feel as if they're actually working for themselves to an extent, Marini says. When your company is acquired—or should it go public—they'll reap the financial benefits of the hard work they've put in for you.

Other perks you can offer your employees include the ability to telecommute on occasion, flexible schedules, education benefits, a casual dress code and employee referral bonuses.

▲

In short, you want to create the kind of environment where you'd like to work. Remember why you went into business for yourself and try to foster the kind of atmosphere you wished for when you worked for someone else.

Not Your Average Perk

Internet startups have a reputation for offering some truly unique employee benefits, from dog-friendly offices to skateboard lanes in the halls. Here are some perks offered by companies attempting to keep their employees happy.

- **A "chill out" room:** This is a place for employees to go and relax during the day. It could include a movie projector or DVD player, video game consoles, and couches or bean bags for lounging around.
- **Massages:** Some companies bring in visiting masseuses to keep employees loose and relaxed. This can either be a short massage session where the entire tab is picked up by the employer or a longer session offered to employees at a discounted rate.
- **Manicures and yoga:** Employees may not have the time to get their nails done or hit the gym, so some companies bring the gym or the nail salon right to their workers. The tab can be picked up either fully or partially by the employer.

Getting
Noticed

Your net service is moving right along; now's the time to grow. One way to do that is through the use of marketing, advertising and public relations. While all these are means of gaining attention for your business, they don't all work the same way.

Many people use the terms advertising and marketing interchangeably, but they're not synonymous. Marketing, which is the overall strategy of finding ways to get your net service noticed by various markets or clients, is comprised of many parts. Advertising, on the other hand, is just one part of your marketing strategy; conducting the market research that we detailed in Chapter 6 is another. PR, which is the process of gaining publicity by reaching out to the press in a nonpaid manner (as opposed to the paid process of advertising) is another part of your overall marketing strategy.

Now, let's talk about how each of these work for your net service.

Marketing

Earlier in this book, we discussed how you should conduct market research before launching your net service. If you listened to us, you likely already have a marketing plan in place—even though you may not know it.

Just what is a marketing plan? Unlike a business plan, a marketing plan focuses on your customers. It includes numbers, facts and objectives, but it's not primarily numerical; it's strategic. It's a plan of action that details what you will sell; to whom you will sell and how often; at what price; and how you will deliver your service to the buyer. Here's a closer look at putting together a marketing plan that works.

- **Step One: Define your product.** In your case, your product is the service you're delivering. The first part of your marketing plan defines your service and its features and benefits, and then explains how it differs from the competition. The more clearly and succinctly you describe your service in your marketing plan, the better you'll be able to communicate that to your target clientele.

  The markets for many net services—especially the crowded ones for SEM firms and new media services—are tough to crack. You need to position your service competitively to break into the market. Doing this requires not just the ability to describe your service but the ability to describe your competitors' services—and explain why yours is better.

  Positioning your service involves two steps. First, you need to analyze the features you're offering and determine how they differentiate your service from those of your competitors. Second, you need to describe what type of buyer is likely to purchase your service. Determining your price and your placement (targeting high-end customers willing to pay more vs. aiming for a lower-end audience who wants a free service, for example) will help you better position your service.

- **Step Two: Describe your target customer.** Developing a profile of your target client is the second step in an effective marketing plan. Try to describe your clients in terms of demographics—age, sex, family composition, earnings and geographic location—as well as lifestyle. The information you gather about the target clientele for your online business is similar to what you'd like to know if your business were offline: What are their hobbies and interests? What do they do in their free time? How do they spend their money?

- **Step Three: Create a communications strategy.** Your target clientele must not only know your product exists but must also have a favorable impression of its benefits. Communication includes everything from logo design and advertising to public relations and promotions. Spell out what you want to accomplish with this strategy (do you want people to recognize your company name, for example?), and find out where you should place your messages.

Advertising

Now that you have a communications strategy in place, it's time to think about advertising, which will likely be a part of that overall strategy. But many of the advertising rules that apply to offline businesses likely won't apply to your net service. Many net service providers don't even think you should advertise; they say your money is better spent on attending trade shows and networking within your industry. We'll discuss these options later in this chapter.

Still, some companies will want to advertise—at least initially. Let's talk about ways you can do that.

Where to Advertise

Your net service lives online, and that's where many of your potential clients spend a good portion of their time. So it stands to reason that advertising online makes sense. Internet advertising also has the advantage of being measurable: When you place an ad online, you can find out how many people click on it. If you place an ad in a magazine or on TV, you can only make educated guesses about how many people actually see it or take notice of it.

One of the first places you might advertise your net service—especially if you're a website designer or a new SEM firm looking to gain experience—is on classified sites like Craigslist. You don't have a whole lot of control over how the ad will look, but in most cases, it's free.

Stat Fact
U.S. online advertising will double by 2011—reaching more than $50 billion in revenue—according to a recent report by the Yankee Group.

If you have an actual advertising budget, you may want to spend some of it on a program like Google AdWords (http://adwords.google.com). AdWords lets you bid on specific keywords, and when users search for those keywords, your ad may run alongside the search results they see. Sound familiar? This is the same process that many SEM firms run for their clients; it's the PPC ad program we discussed earlier in this book.

Also, in Chapter 10, we explained how you can run ads from Google's AdSense program on your site to generate revenue; this is the flip side of that program. AdWords lets you become the advertiser; your company's ad may run on the sites using the AdSense program if you become part of the content network.

Bright Idea

Need to generate a little extra cash at some point, say around the holidays? Try posting a few ads on sites like Craigslist. You don't have to spend anything, and you may attract new clients and generate more business.

Using AdWords—and similar programs like Microsoft's adCenter (http://ad center.microsoft.com) and Yahoo!'s Sponsored Search (http://sem.smallbusiness. yahoo.com/searchenginemarketing)—may sound like a no-brainer, especially for SEM firms that are well-versed in handling these PPC campaigns. But it may not always be your best bet. "We don't use paid search for ourselves," says UpWord SEM's Robert Cavilla. "We tried it, and the quality of leads wasn't very good. We got a lot of people who wanted advice but didn't get a lot of business out of it."

AdWords and similar programs largely use text-based ads. In some cases, you can run image ads, but many AdSense customers prefer to run text-only ads on their sites.

Beware!

Flashy ads that pop up or play sounds may seem like a great way to attract attention. But not all at-tention is good. These kinds of ads risk annoying your potential audience to the point of turning them off of your service.

If you're interested in running image ads—which might make sense if you're launching a splashy new media service, for example—there are various ways to go about it. One is to approach the sites where you think you can find your potential audience, and then ask if they're willing to sell advertising space to you. If you have the budget for it, you may also try approaching big websites—like portals and news providers—and see if they'll sell you space.

Another option for online advertising is link exchanges, where you find sites with similar or complementary products or services and offer to trade links with them. You provide links to their site and vice versa. You can also use e-mail newsletters—especially those targeted to your niche audience—and place advertisements in them.

Offline Advertising for Your Online Business

While your net service startup likely won't be buying a 30-second advertising spot to run during the Super Bowl, that doesn't mean you should rule out offline advertising entirely. Traditional forms of media can offer good exposure for your online business.

Buzz Builders

Online advertisements aren't the only web-based promotional tools at your disposal. Here are a few services you can use to attract attention to your net service.

- **StumbleUpon:** This browser plug-in allows users to discover new websites based on recommendations of other users. If your site hasn't been submitted to the service, you can do so at stumbleupon.com. It's not a surefire way to gain new users, but it's an interesting concept and a lot of fun to use.
- **Digg:** This site, at digg.com, is described as "a place for people to discover and share content from anywhere on the web." Content is submitted by web surfers who find interesting content—whether that's an entire website, a news story, a video or an individual blog post. The site offers a "Digg This" button you can integrate into your site so users can submit your content directly.
- **Del.icio.us:** This is another social bookmarking website, which allows users to save and share favorite links. The site offers a "Save This Page" link that you can add to your site to allow del.icio.us users to save your content directly to their account.

These are only a few of the services available online. You should also submit your site to all major search engines. (Even though all the major search engines are automated and find new sites by crawling the web themselves, you should still submit your site manually.) You'll also want to look at services specific to your industry. Bloggers, for example, should submit their new blogs to blog-specific sites like Technorati (technorati.com), weblogs.com and Blogrolling.com. Website designers and SEO practitioners should consider listing their services in industry-specific directories. Take advantage of all the free resources you can find.

Independent website designers and SEM practitioners who are just starting out and those who wish to target local businesses with their services are especially good candidates for print advertising. Consider your local newspaper, as well as magazines and other publications targeted at your industry.

Any ads you run should contain your (hopefully very-easy-to-remember) URL; you want the people who find your ad to be able to find you online. This is why advertising in a newspaper or a magazine makes more sense than posting billboards on a bus or in a mall, for example. Chances are that people will hold on to the magazine or newspaper, and therefore will still have your ad floating around. An ad posted on the side of a bus or in a mall kiosk is much more fleeting; even if you come up with

Smart Tip

> Tip...

If you run an offline advertisement, make sure your potential clients are able to find you online. They may not remember your company name or URL, but your catchy slogan may have caught their eye. Make sure that when they type that slogan into their favorite search engine, your company shows up in the results.

something snappy enough to grab peoples' attention, what will they remember later that day when they finally sit down at their computer?

Setting Your Budget

If you do decide to advertise, you have to calculate how much you're willing to spend by devoting a percentage of your projected gross sales to your annual advertising budget. Typically, a good rule of thumb is to earmark 2 to 5 percent of your anticipated gross sales for advertising.

There are two primary methods for determining your advertising budget more specifically: the cost method and the task method. The cost method theorizes that an advertiser can't afford to spend more money than he has. Your advertising budget is set strictly as a percentage of your projected gross sales. The task method allows for more flexibility: A company determines how much money will be needed for advertising based on past experience or—in the case of a new startup—based on figures from your business plan and market research.

Remember, though, that the estimate of 2 to 5 percent of gross sales is typical of all types of businesses and is not specific to net services—you may find that advertising isn't the best way to market your net service, so you may want to set your budget lower. Another option is to spend more on advertising when you launch as a way to gain attention initially, and then lower your budget following this "grand opening."

Smart Tip

> Tip...

If your budget allows for it, consider hiring an advertising agency. They can provide expertise and guidance on everything from the content and look of your ads to the best placement and how to evaluate your results.

Getting Publicity

Public relations is the opposite of advertising. In advertising, you pay to have your message placed. With PR, the article that features your company isn't paid for. The reporter, whether print, online or broadcast, reports on your company as a result of information he or she received and researched.

Publicity is more effective than advertising for several reasons. First, it can be far most cost-effective. Second, it has more longevity and the potential to reach a wider

Making the Grade

Not all net services will be subject to reviews in the press, but some—especially new media services—will be. A good review can help your business tremendously; it's a great way to land attention and attract new users. A poor review, however, can hurt—and the sting can last a long time.

"A bad review can kill your site," says Tickle.com's Rick Marini. "A lot of times with the press, you've got one shot. You want to be able to get press around your idea and get people excited, but you can't do that until you're ready to show someone a product that's close to a public launch. If it's clunky, you get a bad review."

The key is timing: You need to let journalists review your site right around the time of your launch, when you're trying to build buzz. You don't want to let them in too early, before you have a service that's performing well. But if you wait too long, you risk missing the window of opportunity.

If your service isn't yet available to the public, you can offer early access to journalists so they can review your offering. But keep Marini's advice in mind: "It's fine to decline review requests. Not all press is good press."

Once your service is publicly available, you don't have the same ability, however. Reporters will be able to access the service, too, so they'll be able to review it more easily. If you're in a public beta—or test—period, the reviews should note that.

audience. Finally—and perhaps most important—it has greater credibility with the public. The audience is likely to believe that if an objective third party, whether it's a newspaper reporter, blogger, magazine writer or TV reporter, is featuring your company, you must be doing something right.

Why do some companies succeed in getting publicity while others don't? The key to securing publicity is to identify your target market and develop a well-thought-out public relations campaign.

Here are some steps you can follow to get your company noticed.

1. **Write your positioning statement.** Sum up in a few sentences what makes your service different from the competition.

2. **List your objectives.** What do you hope to achieve for your company through your publicity plan? Be specific, and set deadlines.

3. **Identify your target customers.** You should already have this information in your marketing plan.

4. **Identify your target media.** List the newspapers, websites, magazines, TV sta-

tions, etc. that would be appropriate outlets. Identify the reporters and editors at those outlets who would be appropriate contacts, and pitch your ideas to them.

5. **Make the pitch.** Put your thoughts on paper or in an e-mail, and send the reporter your pitch. Your pitch may or may not be in the form of a press release; regardless, it should be succinct and include the necessary contact information so the reporter can follow up with you. Never make it difficult for a reporter to figure out who is the appropriate person to contact regarding a press release.

6. **Follow up.** Wait a few days after you've sent your pitch and follow up with a phone call. Do not harass reporters. They receive many, many pitches every day, and if you annoy them, you may find your name crossed off their list.

Talking to the Media

Remember that most reporters you reach are extremely busy and probably on deadline. Be courteous; ask if he or she has time to talk. If not, offer to call back at another time. Keep your initial phone pitch short (20 seconds or less) and offer to send written information as a follow-up.

Here are a few tips for boosting your chances of success.

- If a reporter rejects your idea, you should ask if they can recommend someone else who may be interested.

Beware!
Don't attempt to pitch your idea to all the reporters at a single newspaper or magazine. This isn't likely to increase your chances of coverage; it's more likely to annoy them instead.

- Know exactly what you're going to say when you get the reporter on the telephone, but try not to sound overly scripted.

- Let reporters know you've done your homework and are targeting them based on the beats they cover. For example, you can reference articles they've written recently.

- Be persistent, but don't be a pest. Annoying a reporter isn't going to help your cause.

Hiring Outside Help

If your budget allows for it, hiring an outside public relations agency can help garner publicity for your company. You'll need to budget plenty, though, as this type of relationship can be very expensive.

The benefits of hiring a PR agency are multifold. First, you have an expert craft-

Meet the Press

Think of a press release as your ticket to publicity—one that can get your net service coverage in all kinds of publications. Editors and reporters get hundreds of press releases a day. How do you make yours stand out?

Be sure you have a good reason for sending a press release. A grand opening, a new product or a record-setting sales year are good reasons. You also need to make sure your press release is appropriately targeted for the publication—and the editor—you're sending it to. Don't make the mistake of sending a press release at random.

To ensure readability, your press release should follow the standard format: typed, double-spaced, with a contact person's name, title, company, address and phone number in an easily identifiable location. At the top, you should put a brief, eye-catching headline in bold type. A dateline—for example, "SAN FRANCISCO, March 31, 2008—" follows, leading into the first sentence of the release.

Limit your press release to one or two pages at most. It should be just long enough to cover the six basic elements: who, what, when, where, why and how. The answers to these six questions should be mentioned in order of their importance to the story.

Don't embellish or hype the information. Remember, you're not writing the article; you're merely presenting the information and showing why it's relevant to the publication.

Things to avoid include typos and grammatical mistakes, as well as any attention-grabbing gimmicks. If your press release is well-written and relevant, you don't need singing telegrams to get your message across.

ing your press releases and running your publicity campaigns. These experts have ready-made relationships with the media, so they're likely to be more at ease contacting journalists—and may be more successful at landing your company in the news when they do. Many firms will also offer media training, which can help you and your employees learn how to speak to and deal with the media. Media training is a handy tool if you're interested in positioning yourself as an expert in your field—an excellent idea for any entrepreneur. If you've had media training, you'll sound more polished and feel more comfortable talking on camera, the radio or a podcast.

But outsourcing your public relations needs comes with more than just a financial cost: It will also take a significant amount of your time on an ongoing basis to keep your PR agency up-to-date on your company. They also may not be as knowledgeable about your industry as you or an in-house marketing person might be.

If you're working with a large agency, there's also a good chance that junior-level employees will be handling your account, which could mean you're not getting the expertise you thought you were paying for.

Public relations agencies typically charge monthly fees over a contracted amount of time. A contract may last a year, and the fees can be anywhere from less than $1,000 per month to more than $20,000 per month. The key is to find an agency that meets your needs and offers as much—or as little—service as you need. If you're already comfortable talking to the media, well-versed in writing press releases, and have a good knowledge of the journalists you should be contacting, you may not need an outside PR agency. But if you need the help—and can afford it—hiring an outside PR agency can be an excellent way to increase the publicity your business gets.

As you can see, getting "free" publicity can be costly. But writing press releases and hiring a PR agency aren't the only methods available for boosting your company's image. You should also consider writing articles and blogging as a way of building your reputation.

Building a Reputation as an Author

One of the easiest ways to build your reputation is to become an author. You should write articles that provide insight into your industry and publish them on your own site, as well as in industry newsletters and on your blog. That's right, you—and your business—need a blog. That may sound silly—especially if you're already running a blogging business—but publishing information related to your industry is one of the best ways to establish yourself as a thought leader. And yes, you can blog about the business of blogging.

Blogging about your industry and your specific experiences in it can sell your services to potential clients. Someone looking for advice on optimizing their own website for search engines may come across your SEM blog and realize they need to hire outside help. You don't want your blog to be an advertisement for your company, however; rather, you should use it to discuss trends in the industry, to offer your opinion and to provide advice to newcomers.

The same is true of any types of articles you write for publication. Write as much as you can about your industry and your take on it. Don't think you'll cause yourself to lose business by giving away advice for free; visitors are just as likely to think of you as the established expert if you have so much advice to offer.

In addition to blogging and writing articles, you'll also want to take time to visit the forums and websites you turned to for advice when you were starting out. Go back and become the person who answers questions and provides advice for others.

See Chapter 14 for a list of publications that may accept article submissions and sites that offer forums to post on.

Getting Out: Events and Trade Shows

Writing is one way to get your name out there; another way is to attend industry conferences and trade shows whenever you can. Attending these events is a great way to gain knowledge when you're starting out and to meet and greet people in your industry. As the owner of a new business, one of the most important things you can do is get out of your office (and, in some cases, your pajamas!) and meet people. Attending industry conferences is an excellent way to establish your presence—and that of your company.

As your expertise grows, so should the role you play at these events. You don't want to remain a passive observer, so you should strive to become a panelist or a speaker whenever possible. Get your name, and your company's name, out there by delivering speeches, participating in industry panels and moderating events.

Chapter 14 also has lists of industry events you may want to attend.

Customer Service

Becoming a known expert in your field is another way to grow your reputation, but you also want to make sure you're paying attention to your existing customers. After all, those customers are often the key to new customers: Many net services live off client referrals. One of the most important ways to keep clients happy is by offering first-class customer service.

So what are some of the things you can do to keep your customers happy? One of the biggest things experts recommend is don't make promises you can't keep. That means that an SEM company shouldn't promise first-page placement in search engine rankings if you can't deliver it. A website designer shouldn't promise e-commerce functionality if what you really deliver is good-looking sites. Be honest and upfront with your clients from the beginning to avoid misunderstandings down the road.

Tip...

Smart Tip
As your business grows, your employees may take over the day-to-day tasks of handling your clients. But don't lose touch: Remember that all clients like to hear from the boss every now and then.

Some of these tips may sound basic, but they're worth emphasizing. You need to meet all your deadlines, respond to any questions or concerns in a timely manner, and treat all clients and potential clients with courtesy and respect.

▲

Another way to keep your clients happy: Don't bind them to your service. Many SEM firms require clients to sign a year-long contract up front; Robert Cavilla says that UpWord SEM offers a 30-day out clause. This means if clients aren't happy with the service, they can opt out. You may lose some business this way, but you're also gaining trust and showing your clients that you believe in what you're offering.

You don't want to go overboard to win your clients' love, however. For example, if you're a website designer, you may promise your client a certain number of mock-ups from which he can select the final design of his site. Don't get trapped into providing an endless number of mock-ups; the contract you hand your client should specify exactly how much work you're willing to do in all phases of the project. You need to value your time as much as you value your clients'.

Blogs and new media services may not have paying clients, but they have regular users who must be kept happy. We discussed some of the ways to do this in Chapter 10. Remember: Don't go overboard with annoying ads! If you decide to require your users to register with your site, limit how much information you collect—and guard that information with your life. Nothing generates bad publicity like a breach of sensitive customer information. Make sure your ads target your users; don't waste their time—and that of your advertisers—by displaying irrelevant ads. Users of your new media service or readers of your blog are more likely to mention your service to their friends and colleagues if they're happy with the way they're treated.

For more customer service tips, read the "Now Serving" chapter in *Startup Basics*.

14

Staying
on Top

Now that your net service is up and running, you may think the hard work is done. But in the fast-moving, ever-changing world of technology, you have to stay on top of your industry. You need to keep an eye on your current competition, as well as the competition that doesn't even exist yet.

Reading industry publications is one way to stay current,

▲

but you also have to get out of your office. Whenever possible, you should hit the road and attend events where you can meet colleagues and—at the same time—build your reputation.

Here are some general must-read publications and must-attend trade shows and industry events, followed by important publications, events and sites for each of the four net services we've covered in this book.

General Technology Events

These trade shows and conferences aren't limited to one of the four net services we discuss in this book, nor are they a fit for all net services. Rather, they're general shows worth considering.

- **International Consumer Electronics Show (CESWeb.org):** Commonly known as CES, this is the behemoth; it's the largest trade show in North America. It occurs each January in Las Vegas and attracts thousands of technology companies as exhibitors and hundreds of thousands of visitors. It's easy to get lost in such an enormous show (the Consumer Electronics Association, which runs the show, estimates that more than 20,000 products were launched at the last show), but it's also a great opportunity to meet and greet.

- **DEMO (demo.com):** This is a selective event that takes place two times a year—once in February and once in September. Startup companies must apply to be an exhibitor, and if they're one of the few selected, they must pay a hefty fee ($18,500 at the last show) to attend. It's considered a prestigious platform through which to launch your company, product or service in front of journalists, venture capitalists and technology industry insiders.

- **CeBIT (cebit.de):** If your business has international appeal, you may want to consider heading overseas to the annual CeBIT show, held each spring in Hannover, Germany. It's billed as the largest technology trade show in the world (yes, it's bigger than CES), and it attracts visitors and exhibitors from all over the world.

General Technology Publications

To stay current on everything related to your industry, you need to stay up-to-date on the news surrounding the tech industry as a whole. This means reading newspapers like *The Wall Street Journal* and *The New York Times*, and magazines like *Wired* on a regular basis, but it also means perusing the web regularly. Sites like TechCrunch (techcrunch.com), Techmeme (techmeme.com), CNet's News.com (news.com) and

> ### ⚠ Beware!
> The Consumer Electronics Show is big—and we mean really big. It can be difficult for a startup to get noticed at such a giant show. Should you decide to publicly launch your company at the show and if things go wrong, it could mean failure on a very big stage.

GigaOM (gigaom.com) provide industry news and analysis. Blogs like Engadget (engadget.com) and Gizmodo (gizmodo.com) are more product-heavy but provide a good way to learn about upcoming gadgets and devices.

Industry-Specific Resources

The events and publications listed above are just a few of the technology industry's best resources. As a new business, you may want to consider a smaller event tailored to your specific field, or websites and publications that focus only on your industry. Listed below are specific resources for each type of net service we cover.

Website Design
Industry Events and Conferences

- **SXSW Interactive (sxsw.com):** This "festival" coincides with the SXSW Music Festival that is held each March in Austin, Texas. It's designed for web entrepreneurs and technology companies with a creative bent.

> ### 📈 Stat Fact
> As many as 86 percent of the attendees at a technology trade show have an influence on buying decisions, according to a recent survey by Exhibit Surveys.

- **Web Directions (webdirections.org):** This Australia-based industry group sponsors two conferences each year. Web Directions North is held in Vancouver, Canada, and Web Directions South takes place in Sydney, Australia.

- **An Event Apart (aneventapart.com):** Run by the founder of *A List Apart* magazine (see info on the following page), these conferences take place in various cities throughout the country. The conferences are aimed at designers, developers and anyone interested in gaining a deeper understanding of web standards.

There are many, many smaller industry conferences and events. If you can't afford to travel to the bigger events, look for less-publicized events closer to you. It's worth networking within your industry on whatever scale you can afford.

t won't surprise you to hear that many of the must-read publications for web designers are actually other websites. Many designers turn to blogs and forums to gather and trade knowledge. They also study online galleries of work to learn new skills and gain inspiration for their own designs.

We've compiled a list of recommended sites below. Some are industry publications, and others are industry awards—all showcase innovative website designs. Many web designers study them for inspiration, as we mentioned above, but others strive to get their sites shown on these galleries because they feel it's a badge of honor.

- **A List Apart (alistapart.com):** An online magazine that "explores the design, development and meaning of web content, with a special focus on web standards and best practices."

- **CSSRemix.com:** This site offers a gallery of what it calls "the best designed Web 2.0 sites." You can submit your site for consideration.

- **Stylevault (stylevault.net):** This site offers a showcase for designers to show off their work and get inspired by other talented designers. Like CSSRemix, it allows you to submit sites for inclusion.

Hit the Road

You know that attending industry events is a great way to network in your field. But not all events are the same. Do you know the difference between a trade show and an industry conference? Here's a brief overview of each type of event.

- **Trade Shows:** This is a gathering, often quite large, of companies in a specific industry. Companies rent exhibition space and typically set up a booth offering information on their products and/or services. Trade shows are attended by investors, potential clients, and journalists and analysts covering your industry. Displaying at a trade show can be expensive, but it also can give you the opportunity to reach a vast new audience.

- **Conferences:** Many trade shows run scheduled conferences alongside the show itself. Conferences are composed of sessions, such as panel discussions and seminars, related to a specific industry or field. They are typically a way to gain insight and become educated about an industry. A blogging conference, for example, could include sessions with experts who offer advice on everything from tips on specific blogging platforms to ways to optimize your blog for search engines.

- **CoolHomepages (coolhomepages.com):** This online resource for web designers also showcases sites that it deems remarkable for their design. If your site is showcased here, you can post an award on your site letting your visitors know.

- **Webby Awards (webbyawards.com):** Famous for its five-word acceptance speech policy, the Webbys were established in 1996 (during the web's infancy) and are presented by the International Academy of Digital Arts and Sciences, a 550-member organization that includes celebrities, web experts and businesspeople. Awards are presented annually and include more than 100 categories in four main areas: Websites, Interactive Advertising, Online Film & Video and Mobile.

SEM

Industry Events and Conferences

- **Search Engine Strategies (searchenginestrategies.com):** A series of conferences that take place in cities all over the world, including London, Chicago, New York and San Jose, California.

- **Search Marketing Expo (searchmarketingexpo.com):** A conference organized by Third Door Media, the company that also offers the Search Engine Land website (see below). SMX conferences take place all over the globe.

Industry Publications, Associations and Awards

- **Search Engine Guide (searchengineguide.com):** This site calls itself "an educational website aimed at translating the search marketing world into something that small-business owners can understand."

- **Search Engine Land (searchengineland.com):** This site offers "must-read news about search marketing and search engines."

- **Search Engine Roundtable (SEORoundtable.com):** This unique website aggregates information posted on SEM-related forums "to provide a single source for the reader to visit to locate the most interesting threads covered at the SEM forums."

- **Search Engine Watch (searchenginewatch.com):** This robust site offers search engine tips and information, statistics, expert commentary, and forums where users can post questions and swap information.

- **Search Engine Marketing Professional Organization (sempo.org):** A non-profit organization that serves the SEM market, SEMPO offers a directory of SEM providers, industry research, articles on the SEM field, information on SEO/SEM committees and working groups, and educational resources.

- **SEO Book (SEObook.com):** A blog that covers the SEO and SEM industry, this site also offers training programs, a collection of tools for SEO/SEM practitioners and a calendar of useful industry events.

- *SEO Consultants Directory* (**SEO-consultants.com**): This site offers a listing of professional SEO and SEM providers. It's free to be listed, but companies that are listed have been reviewed and approved by the editorial staff.

- **SEOmoz** (**seomoz.org**): This Seattle-based SEO company provides "a hub for search marketers worldwide." The site offers industry-related news and blogs, as well as a collection of tools for SEO providers. The company also gives out "Web 2.0 awards" each year to sites that excel in demonstrating Web 2.0 characteristics.

> ⚠️ **Beware!**
> The Webby Awards are often dominated by big name companies. Recent winners include *The New Yorker*, Greenpeace, Toyota and *The New York Times*. So don't be discouraged if you don't win an award yourself. See what you can learn from the sites that are honored.

New Media Service
Industry Events and Conferences

The list of industry conferences and events that may pertain to your new media service is vast; your new media service, after all, can be almost anything. You may want to consider the Consumer Electronics Show, the DEMO conference and the SXSW Interactive festival we mentioned earlier in this chapter. Other events worth considering include:

- **Dow Jones Web Ventures (webventures.dowjones.com):** This event is designed to bring investors and entrepreneurs together. It includes panel presentations and keynotes from venture capitalists, and allows startups the chance to present their business plans to an audience of investors.

- **Digital Experience (digfocus.com /digitalhome):** This is an event held for the media on the eve of the Consumer Electronics Show. Companies present their products and services to a more exclusive audience of journalists and analysts; the public is not allowed to attend, and the event is more intimate than the giant show itself.

- **DigitalLife (digitallife.com):** This

> 💡 **Bright Idea**
> Don't forget to take advantage of the local business associations in your area. Join your local chamber of commerce, or check out smaller technology groups that may be nearby.

show, which takes place in New York City in the fall, showcases technology, gaming, and entertainment products and services designed for consumers.

- **Web 2.0 Summit (web2summit.com):** Held each fall in San Francisco, this event includes a "LaunchPad," an event that—like DEMO—allows a select group of startups to demonstrate their product or service in front of a panel of VCs.

- **Web 2.0 Expo (web2expo.com):** A companion event to the Web 2.0 Summit, this is a conference and trade show for the many folks who are "embracing the opportunities created by Web 2.0 technologies," including designers, developers, product managers, entrepreneurs, VCs, marketers and business strategies. It's held twice a year: once in San Francisco and once in New York City. The event is co-produced by TechWeb (techweb.com) and O'Reilly Media (oreilly.com), which was founded by Tim O'Reilly, who, as we explained in Chapter 1, is credited with inventing the term "Web 2.0."

- **New Media Expo (newmediaexpo.com):** A convention for online audio and video creators, this event aims to offer hands-on and how-to sessions that allow attendees to gain knowledge and skills.

Industry Publications, Associations and Awards

Just as the industry events that pertain to your new media service will vary, so too will the publications, associations and awards that might interest you. In general, you should keep up-to-date on the tech industry in general by using the blogs and sites we listed earlier, including TechCrunch, Techmeme, Engadget and Gizmodo. Other publications to consider include:

> ⚠ **Beware!**
> Many publications and websites also hand out awards of dubious distinction: worst-of lists. You can't do anything to prevent your company from earning this type of award—other than offering top-notch service, of course. But you can try to learn from the bad reviews you get.

- **Mashable (mashable.com):** This blog is devoted to social networking news.

- **Webware (webware.com):** CNET runs this blog that covers Web 2.0 applications. It also offers the Webware 100 awards, designed to honor its readers' favorite Web 2.0 services and applications.

Other industry publications offer awards as well. CNET.com hands out its "Best of CES" awards at the giant technology show every year, while *PC World* magazine publishes an annual list of the "100 Best Products of the Year."

▲

Blogging Business
Industry Events and Conferences

- **BlogWorld & New Media Expo (blogworldexpo.com):** This trade show and conference is designed for people who are blogging, vlogging (video blogging), podcasting and producing new media content.

- **SOBCon (sobevent.com):** Also known as the Successful and Outstanding Bloggers Conference, this event calls itself a "biz school for bloggers." It's designed for both entrepreneurs and corporate bloggers. The program says it will "send each attendee home with a Business Action Plan that can be immediately executed for measurable success."

- **WordCamp (wordcamp.org):** This blogging conference focuses on the WordPress application and its users. Events are held around the world and in U.S. cities; the last event was held outside Dallas.

Industry Publications, Associations and Awards

- **Bloggies (bloggies.com):** These weblog awards are handed out annually at the South by Southwest Interactive Festival in Austin, Texas. They honor the "best of" blogs in a variety of topics.

- **BlogHer (blogher.com):** This online community for women bloggers also hosts the annual BlogHer conference.

- **ProBlogger (problogger.net):** A blog devoted to the business of blogging, ProBlogger offers tips on how to generate revenue, improve your blog content and promote your blog.

Do's and Don'ts

Launching your net service may seem like a daunting process. It will be a lot of work, sure, but there is much to gain from it, too. And you can make the process of building your company fun and rewarding. Here's some expert advice and a few tips on what you should and shouldn't do throughout all the stages of launching your company.

▲

DO: Dream—and plan—as big or as small as you'd like. If you're interested in starting a one-man, part-time web design shop, that's great. But if your plan is to create the next Facebook, that's great, too.

DO: Make sure you have a plan to generate revenue, not just a plan to attract eyeballs to your website.

DON'T: Dump too much money into your blog—or any type of net service—before you've verified that a market exists. "If you start a blog, give it three to six months to see how it's doing before you put too much money into marketing it. If you can get to 1,000 visitors a day, you know a market exists and you can justify spending money on advertising on sites like Facebook and Google," says Rob May, the blogger behind BusinessPundit.com.

DO: Pick a name you like, and make sure you're legally cleared to use it. Changing your name midstream can hurt your business.

DO: Work for free when you first start out. "Give your work away until you're ready to charge people," says James Paden, an Indianapolis-based web developer. Design or optimize sites (if your field is SEO) for friends, neighbors and nonprofits; gain experience however you can.

DO: Charge a fee that reflects the level of service you're delivering to your clients. "I realize how much I value my time, and I know what kind of return I'm making for people," says SEO consultant Todd Mailcoat.

> **Tip...**
>
> **Smart Tip**
>
> Make sure you have a business plan. Entrepreneurs who take the time to write a formal plan are more likely to actually create their business rather than abandoning their idea during the planning stages.

DON'T: Cave in and lower your rate if you think your time is worth more than that.

DO: Raise your rates when you believe it's justified.

DON'T: "Try to monetize your blog [or website] too soon. You need to let your audience grow to a decent level. Establish a connection with your audience, and they'll be more receptive to advertising," says May.

DON'T: "Waste good content space on bad ads," says Tickle.com's Rick Marini.

DO: Try to work regular business hours, even as a sole proprietor, so that you treat your freelance gig with the seriousness and professionalism you would give to any job. Even if you're working from your home, you should get up each morning and get dressed as if you were going into an office. You're more likely to be productive that way.

DO: Recognize your own limitations, and find partners and employees who offer skills that are complementary to your own.

A History Lesson

Before you launch your net service, we have one more suggestion for you: You should recall the bursting of the dotcom bubble.

Why would you want to think about the mass failure of internet companies just when you're getting ready to launch one? Taking a look at the many reasons why the bubble burst and which companies managed to survive can provide you with a few tips on what you should—and shouldn't—do with your own internet business.

"Today, there's some level of historical perspective" to the internet, says Jon Gibs, vice president of media analytics with Nielsen Online. He says there are two major differences between today's dotcom business market and that of the pre-bubble days: "First, there's not quite the same glut of capital, and, second, there's not quite the same glut of really terrible ideas."

Another difference with today's market is that companies typically don't fail on as big a scale as they did in the past, Gibs says. "Small companies may have reasonably good ideas. They go through business planning, maybe angel investing. If their idea doesn't pan out, they just slowly fade away. Companies today don't really become as big. They slowly disappear, as opposed to the colossal flameouts we saw in the past," he says.

What can you do to prevent your business from fading away? Going through all the planning and preparation stages that we've recommended in this book is a good start.

DON'T: Hire people you don't like. "Keeping the jerks out is a big deal," Marini says. You're going to be spending a lot of time with your employees, so make sure you'll really enjoy being around them.

DO: Become a thought leader in your industry, says Robert Cavilla of UpWord SEM. When you're just starting out, you should attend industry conferences to gain knowledge; later on, you should strive to become a speaker at those same events.

Stat Fact
About 7 percent of the working age population in the United States is "actively engaged in efforts to start a new business" in any given year, says the SBA.

DO: Get involved with local business and networking groups.

DON'T: Let your internet-based business cut you off from society around you.

▲

DO: Dig a little deeper than your competition, especially if you're blogging. "There aren't a lot of bloggers who have the time or the interest to dig deep into things," May says. Doing some research into the topics that other bloggers are glossing over can lead to more interesting content for your blog—and more readers, too.

DO: Make sure you're entering a field you'll enjoy, not just one that will make you money.

DO: Have passion for your business. "You have to be fired up every day," Marini says. "You have to love what you do every day."

You may not make millions, but if you love what you do, you've found success.

Glossary

Advertising network: a company that connects advertisers with publishers that want to display ads

Affiliate programs: a program that allows companies to earn revenue by advertising and selling the products of another company

AJAX (Asynchronous JavaScript and XML): a group of related web technologies used to create interactive web applications

Angel investor: a private individual who invests his or her own money into an entrepreneurial company; angels can be affiliated (meaning they're familiar with you or your business beforehand) or nonaffiliated

Blog: short for weblog, a blog is an online journal with a series of entries that are posted in reverse chronological order

Copyright: legal protection offered by the government to guard original works of authorship

CPC (cost-per-click): a method of advertising that pays money to the publisher only when an online ad is clicked on by a site visitor

▲

CPM (cost-per-thousand): a method of advertising in which advertisers pay website publishers a certain amount of money for every 1,000 ads displayed on their website(s)

CSS (Cascading Style Sheets): a language that's used to style web pages; it takes the information in the markup language used to build a website (such as HTML or XML) and presents it to the user

Crawler: software used by search engines to examine the content of websites and determine whether a particular site matches a search query

Debt financing: receiving money to start or run your business in the form of a loan you have to repay

Domain name: the name that a company or individual registers to use as a location on the internet

Equity financing: receiving money to start or run your business in exchange for an ownership stake

Errors & Omissions: insurance that protects you against liability for damages caused to your clients by any errors or omissions in the service you deliver

Flash: multimedia technology that allows you to add interactive and animated components to a website

FTP (file transfer protocol): protocol used to exchange files between computers over the internet

Google AdSense: Google's ad network for website publishers; it allows you to earn revenue by displaying ads from AdWords users

Google AdWords: a network that allows advertisers to sell their ads to publishers who use Google's AdSense program; it also allows advertisers to bid on keywords; when users search Google for those keywords, their ad will appear alongside the results if they have bid enough for it

HTML (HyperText Markup Language): a markup language that allows you to create web pages

JavaScript: a programming language that allows you to create applets, which are applications that run in a web browser as part of the content on a web page

Keywords: terms that advertisers bid on through PPC (pay-per-click) ad programs like Google AdWords; keywords are also terms used on a web page that factor into its search engine ranking

Mashup: a web application that allows the user to mix content from more than one website

Media liability: a form of insurance that protects publishers from claims involved with communicating information to the public, including defamation and infringement

Metadata: data that describes the content and purpose of a web page, including its keywords; metadata is typically contained in tags that are invisible to web users

Open source: a development method for software in which the source code is freely available and can be modified

Patent: legal protection offered by the government to protect inventors; a patent excludes others from making, using or selling your invention in the United States

Podcasting: to record audio or video files, and make them available online so they can be downloaded and listened to or viewed by users; most podcasts are also available as subscriptions, with regular updates delivered to the audience via a "podcatching client" like Apple's iTunes or Microsoft's Zune Marketplace

PHP (Hypertext Preprocessor): a web programming language that allows for the creation of dynamic content that can interact with databases

RSS feed: a family of web feed formats, specified in XML and used for web syndication

SEM (search engine marketing): the process of increasing traffic to a website through paid methods, such as the pay-per-click ad programs AdWords and adCenter

SEO (search engine optimization): the process of optimizing the content of a website, including its use of keywords, to improve its listing in search engine results organically

Service mark: a word, name or symbol that's used to identify and distinguish the services offered by one company from those offered by another

Social bookmarking: websites and services that allow users to save their favorite web pages and share them with others

Social networking: websites and services that link people together and allow them to connect with one another

TrackBack: a system that allows a conversation of sorts between two blogs; when one blogger writes a post about another person's blog, their posting also appears as a comment on the original blog site; both the blog post and the comment link to one another, allowing readers of each blog to discover the other one

Trademark: a word, name or symbol that's used to identify and distinguish one company from another

URL (uniform resource locator): the address of documents or web pages located on the World Wide Web

Venture capital: a type of equity capital, in which a group of professionals invests in a company

World Wide Web: a series of interlinked hypertext documents (web pages) that are accessed via the internet

Web 2.0: a term used to denote a turning point in the history of the web, marked by more user interaction with the web, as well as more user-created content

Web designer: someone who creates the graphics and content that contributes to the look and feel of a website

Web developer: someone who builds a website using programming languages; they're responsible for the framework behind the content you see on a web page

Widget: miniature web applications that allow users to view information such as news headlines or weather forecasts, view photos, and play music and video

Wiki: a collaborative website that allows readers to add content on a subject, which can also be edited by others; Wikipedia is a good example of a Wiki site

XML (Extensible Markup Language): a markup language that was designed to transport data, as opposed to displaying it, as HTML does

Appendix
Net Services
Resources

You know how quickly things change in today's Web 2.0 world, so it won't surprise you to hear that your best resources are the ones that can constantly be updated. The web itself is, of course, one of the best places to learn innovative techniques and study new technologies that have the possibility to revolutionize your business. But sorting out the gems from the junk online can be a challenge, so we've

▲

put together a list of some of the best sites and services for you. Our list of resources goes beyond websites and services, though—something you should keep in mind when planning your net service. There's plenty that you can learn in the offline world as well.

Accounting and Bookkeeping Tools

FreshBooks
invoicing and time-tracking service
freshbooks.com

Intuit Online Payroll
payroll.intuit.com

Microsoft Office Accounting
microsoft.com/office/accounting

MYOB Premier Accounting
myob-us.com

NetSuite Small Business
hosted accounting, CRM and business management software
netsuite.com

PayCycle Payroll Plus
paycycle.com

Peachtree Accounting
Sage Software
peachtree.com

QuickBooks
quickbooks.com

Quicken
quicken.intuit.com

Advertising and Affiliate Programs

24/7 Real Media
247realmedia.com

AdBrite
adbrite.com

Amazon Associates
affiliate marketing program
affiliate-program.amazon.com/gp/associates/join

BlogAds
blogads.com

Burst Media
burstmedia.com

Chitika
chitika.com

CrispAds
crispads.com

eBay Partner Network
affiliate marketing program
ebaypartnernetwork.com

Google AdSense
google.com/adsense

Google AdWords
google.com/adwords

Kanoodle
kanoodle.com

Blogging Software and Services

b2evolution
b2evolution.net

Blogger
blogger.com

Bloogz
bloogz.com

Google BlogSearch
blogsearch.google.com

LifeType
lifetype.net

Movable Type
movabletype.com

Technorati
technorati.com

Textpattern
textpattern.com

TypePad
typepad.com

WordPress
installed server application
wordpress.org

▲

Business Planning and Market Research Tools

Alexa
alexa.com

Business Plan Pro
paloalto.com

PlanHQ
planhq.com

PlanWrite for Business
brs-inc.com

Whois
domain name lookup
whois.net

Business Software Services

Basecamp
project management and collaboration software
basecamphq.com

Drive Headquarters
online backup and storage
drivehq.com

ElephantDrive
online storage and off-site data back up
elephantdrive.com

Google Apps
google.com/a

Microsoft Office Live Workspace
officelive.com

Microsoft Office Small Business
office.microsoft.com

OpenOffice
openoffice.org

ThinkFree Office Online
thinkfree.com

Trillian Universal Instant Messenger
ceruleanstudios.com

Xdrive
online storage
xdrive.com

Zoho Office Suite
zoho.com

Domain Name Registrars

Go Daddy
godaddy.com

Network Solutions
networksolutions.com

Register.com
register.com

Financial Resources

Payscale Salary Survey
payscale.com

PayPal
paypal.com

Sales Tax Institute
salestaxinstitute.com

Yetter Consulting Services
sales and use tax guidance
ycstax.com

Financing/Investors

Active Capital
activecapital.org

Charles River Ventures
crv.com/quickstart

Directory of Angel Investors
Gaebler Ventures
gaebler.com/angel-investor-networks.htm

Entrepreneur's Top 100 Venture Capital Firms
entrepreneur.com/vc100

LendingClub
online lending network
lendingclub.com

National Venture Capital Association
nvca.com

▲

Prosper
person-to-person lending network
prosper.com

Freelancers/Homebased Entrepreneurs

Contract Worker
contract-worker.com

Freelancers Union
freelancersunion.org

Guru.com
guru.com

SitePoint
sitepoint.com

Government Resources

SBA
sba.gov

U.S. Copyright Office
copyright.gov

U.S. Patent and Trademark Office
uspto.gov

Insurance

eHealth Insurance
ehealthinsurance.com

Freelancers Union
freelancersunion.org

Media/Professional Insurance
mediaprof.com

National Association for the Self-Employed
nase.org

Techinsurance
techinsurance.com

New Media Software

Apple Dashboard Widgets
apple.com/downloads/dashboard

Clearspring Community Platform
platform for building, deploying and monetizing widgets
clearspring.com

Google Gadgets
code.google.com/apis/gadgets

Google Gadget Ventures
a program that offers grants and investments to gadget developers
google.com/gadgetventures

MySQL
open-source database application
mysql.com

PHP
scripting language for web development
php.net

Ruby on Rails
open-source web development framework
rubyonrails.org

WidgetBox
platform for developers to share their widgets
widgetbox.com

Yahoo! Widgets
widgets.yahoo.com

Search Engine Marketing Organizations and Online Resources

Search Engine Guide
searchengineguide.com

Search Engine Land
searchengineland.com

Search Engine Roundtable
seoroundtable.com

Search Engine Watch
searchenginewatch.com

SEMPO (Search Engine Marketing Professional Organization)
sempo.org

SEO Book
seobook.com

▲

SEO Consultants Directory
seoconsultants.com

SEOmoz
seomoz.org

Stuntdubl
stuntdubl.com

Search Engine Marketing Software and Services

ClickTracks
website analytics software
clicktracks.com

Compete
competitive search metrics and site analysis
compete.com

Google Analytics
site analytics
google.com/analytics

Google Trends
keyword research tool
google.com/trends

Google Directory
source of links for websites
google.com/dirhp

Hitwise
competitive analysis tool
hitwise.com

KeywordDiscovery.com
keyword research tool
keyworddiscovery.com

Omniture
web analytics software
omniture.com

WebPosition
search engine optimization and marketing software
webposition.com

WebTrends
web analytics and statistics software
webtrends.com

Wordtracker.com
keyword research tool
wordtracker.com

Xenu Link Sleuth
link building and repair tool
home.snafu.de/tilman/xenulink.html

Website Design Software

Adobe Acrobat 8.0 Professional
adobe.com

Adobe Creative Suite 4 Web Standard
includes CS4 versions of Dreamweaver, Flash Professional, Fireworks, Contribute, Adobe Bridge, Version Cue, Adobe Device Central and Adobe Connect
adobe.com

CorelDraw Graphics Suite X4
includes applications for creating digital illustrations; editing photos; creating web and print layouts; and tracing bitmap images
corel.com

Microsoft Expression Web
web design application
microsoft.com/expression

Website Designer Publications and Directories

A List Apart
alistapart.com

Stylevault
stylevault.net

CoolHomepages
coolhomepages.com

Xemion Web Designer Directory
xemion.com

Technology Blogs and News Sites

CNET News.com
news.com

Engadget
engadget.com

▲

GigaOM
http://gigaom.com

Gizmodo
http://gizmodo.com

Mashable
http://mashable.com

TechCrunch
techcrunch.com

Techmeme
techmeme.com

Webware
webware.com

Wired magazine
wired.com

Trade Shows and Conferences

CeBIT
cebit.de

BlogWorld & New Media Expo
blogworldexpo.com

DEMO
demo.com

International CES (Consumer Electronics Show)
cesweb.org

Search Engine Strategies
searchenginestrategies.com

Search Marketing Expo (SMX)
searchmarketingexpo.com

SXSW Interactive
sxsw.com

Web Directions
webdirections.org

Web 2.0 Summit
web2summit.com

Web 2.0 Expo
web2expo.com

Index